Authentic Academic Leadership

Authentic Academic Leadership

A Values-Based Approach to College Administration

Jeffrey L. Buller

ROWMAN & LITTLEFIELD
Lanham • Boulder • New York • London

Published by Rowman & Littlefield
An imprint of The Rowman & Littlefield Publishing Group, Inc.
4501 Forbes Boulevard, Suite 200, Lanham, Maryland 20706
https://rowman.com

Unit A, Whitacre Mews, 26-34 Stannary Street, London SE11 4AB,
United Kingdom

Copyright © 2018 by Jeffrey L. Buller

All rights reserved. No part of this book may be reproduced in any form or by any electronic or mechanical means, including information storage and retrieval systems, without written permission from the publisher, except by a reviewer who may quote passages in a review.

British Library Cataloguing in Publication Information Available

Library of Congress Cataloging-in-Publication Data Available

ISBN 978-1-4758-4243-2 (cloth : alk. paper)
ISBN 978-1-4758-4244-9 (pbk. : alk. paper)
ISBN 978-1-4758-4245-6 (electronic)

♾ ™ The paper used in this publication meets the minimum requirements of American National Standard for Information Sciences Permanence of Paper for Printed Library Materials, ANSI/NISO Z39.48-1992.

Printed in the United States of America

To Warren Jones ("The Dean of the World"), former Dean of Arts and Sciences at Georgia Southern University, one of the most principled, values-based, and authentic academic leaders I have known

Contents

Introduction

If once a man indulges himself in murder, very soon he comes to think little of robbing; and from robbing he comes next to drinking and Sabbath-breaking, and from that to incivility and procrastination. Once begun upon this downward path, you never know where you are to stop. Many a man has dated his ruin from some murder or other that perhaps he thought little of at the time.

— Thomas De Quincey, *Murder Considered as One of the Fine Arts* (1827/2006) 45

Authentic leadership means surprisingly different things to different people. I've attended presentations that people have given on what they call authentic leadership that dealt with matters so far removed from what I'll be talking about in this book that I couldn't even recognize their topics as remotely related to mine.

So, let me make clear at the outset a point that will be developed throughout the pages that follow: By *authentic leadership*, I mean leadership that genuinely stems from your own core values. Those values may be different from those of everyone else you know, they may be identical, or (as is usually the case) they will overlap with those of others to some degree and be distinctly your own to some degree.

Moreover, as I'll elaborate in chapter 5, your values, perspective, or core beliefs don't have to be limited to those qualities that others admire or that are generally socially acceptable. In the sense that I mean it, authentic leadership is about knowing who you are, owning that identity, and acting genuinely in accordance with that identity.

Authentic leaders, whether in higher education or other walks of life, know what they stand for and embody those convictions in their actions. If compassion and concern for others is important to them, they act in genuinely caring and compassionate ways. And if they're SOBs, at least you know they're SOBs; they don't try to hide it, and they don't pretend to be anything else. You can hate what they stand for, but at least they stand for something, and they're not hypocrites.

For this reason, there are entire schools of thought about authenticity and authentic leadership that you won't find addressed in these pages. Among these intentional omissions are the following:

- The approach to authentic leadership taken by the Authentic Leadership Center at Naropa University (Authentic Leadership Center, 2017), which includes many elements of other approaches, such as mindful leadership and servant leadership, each of which is valuable and important in itself but, when combined with what I and many others regard as authentic leadership, tends to cloud the picture.

- Marshall Berman whose *Politics of Authenticity* (1970) traced the modern concept of authenticity to eighteenth-century France and viewed it as a reaction against bourgeois capitalism's pre-occupation with self-interest and ultimately the consumer culture of the later western world.

- Andrew Potter who was much influenced by Berman and whose *The Authenticity Hoax* (2010) argues that much of what currently passes for individualism and "being oneself" is really just self-absorption and, in an ironic turn on Berman, supported by a consumer culture that sells people the outward trappings of their "individual" identities.

- What we might call Commercial Authenticity Variation A, the quest for "pure," "natural," and "genuine" ingredients in the products we buy, as discussed in such works as James H. Gilmore and B. Joseph Pine's *Authenticity: What Consumers Really Want* (2007).

- What we might call Commercial Authenticity Variation B, the movement by certain advertisers to convey a more "genuine" marketing message through the use of real people instead of actors in their advertisements, the effort to be "sincere" and unpretentious in corporate communications, and to avoid anything that may be seen as hype or exaggeration. This sense of the word *authenticity* is discussed by such authors as Ron Willingham in *Authenticity: The Head, Heart, and Soul of Selling* (2014).

- Other approaches that insist that leaders must have specific traits or adopt certain leadership styles in order to be considered "authentic," such as Kevin Kruse's conclusion (based on his reading of other authors) that all authentic leaders are mission driven and focused on results (Kruse, 2013), Trent Keough's belief that all ap-

proaches to authenticity have been historically based in a commitment to truth, trust, reality, and authority and are a reaction against
some or all of their contemporaries whom they regard as "inauthentic" (Keough, 2017), or R. Michael Anderson's notion that all
authentic leaders are motivated by a vision (Anderson, 2015).

You may also encounter other idiosyncratic definitions of authentic
leadership—and they, along with the approaches summarized above, are
not without some degree of interest and value—but the point is that
they're not relevant to my subject here. For me, in the pages that follow,
the word *authenticity* is going to mean nothing more and nothing less
than being true to a small set of key values or principles that define who
you are and guide your actions.

As we'll see in chapter 1, this notion does indeed have an interesting
philosophical and historical basis, but many people are authentic academic leaders without mastering all the complex concepts and systems
that we encounter in many books and workshops on authenticity. They
are just themselves, and this book is intended to provide a pathway back
to ourselves for those of us who, to paraphrase Dante, midway through
the journey of our lives find ourselves in a dark forest, having lost the
straight path.

There are many people to thank for their assistance throughout the
creation of this book, including:

- All those who attended my daylong workshops on Authentic Academic Leadership, both here in the United States and in Saudi Arabia; your conversations, corrections, and questions guided what
began as a very rough and inchoate concept into what I believe is
now a useful tool for improving leadership in higher education.
- Kim Strom-Gottfried, the chief integrity officer at the University of
North Carolina at Chapel Hill for the many engaging conversations
on values-based academic leadership during our presentations in
Abha, Khobar, Qassim, and Hail.
- My colleague in ATLAS, Bob Cipriano, who is endlessly valuable as
a sounding board for ideas. He's perhaps the only person I've ever
met to whom I can say, "Let's go to lunch and, as we talk, see if we
can come up with a list of every value, virtue, or principle in higher
education we can think of" (something I actually said to him), not

receive a puzzled look in response, and be told only, "Sounds like fun. Let's do it."

- ATLAS's graphic designer, Dana Babbs, who designed figures 1.2, 3.2, 4.1, and 6.1 and gave me permission to reproduce them here.

- Rebecca Peter, my editorial assistant in Florida Atlantic University's Leadership and Professional Development Program, who also served as a research assistant for this book. The pages that follow are much richer in ideas and much freer of typographical and grammatical idiosyncrasies because of her contributions.

I should mention one other relationship in the interest of full disclosure. In chapter 1, I list a number of situations in which the values of college leaders were tested and found lacking. Among the examples I cite is Graham Spanier, the former president of Pennsylvania State University.

Graham is a personal friend and, in my opinion, one of the kindest and most principled leaders (academic or otherwise) whom I've ever met. I fully concur with the opinion of Stanley Ikenberry (also a colleague) who stated in *The Chronicle of Higher Education*, "The Graham Spanier I know is a person of considerable ability but also a person of considerable humanity. . . . I saw that before, during his presidency, and I've seen it afterward. He's a person of character and compassion" (Stripling, 2017, A31).

I have included Graham in this list because I believe the Pennsylvania State University case represents a situation in which the values of academic leaders were widely scrutinized and, in retrospect, found to be questionable. In my personal opinion, however, I believe that Graham Spanier was someone who sincerely was trying to make the best possible decision for all concerned, based on the information available to him at the time.

As a cautionary tale, it reminds us just how challenging many of these value judgments are and how easy it is for those not involved in them to decide in hindsight, when more information is available, what should or should not have been done.

Authentic academic leadership is a topic that has been an ongoing interest of mine and one that reflects my personal view of what higher education is for: not merely preparing people for jobs and increasing economic capital, but also preparing people for life and increasing intellectual, cultural, and civic capital. While I'm enough of a post-modernist to distrust any sweeping generalizations about universal values and unchanging truths, I'm also enough of a traditionalist to believe that each of us needs to seek (and again in my opinion) *create* the meaning of our lives, work, and interactions with others.

Whether you're a universalist, a relativist, or somewhere in between, I hope you'll find these reflections on authentic academic leadership useful in helping you develop a leadership approach that flows consistently from your own core values.

REFERENCES

Anderson, R. M. (June 16, 2015). 5 steps to becoming an authentic leader. *Entrepreneur*. https://www.entrepreneur.com/article/246661.

Authentic Leadership Center: Naropa University. (2017). http://www.naropa.edu/academics/alc/.

Berman, M. (1970). *The politics of authenticity: Radical individualism and the emergence of modern society*. New York: Atheneum.

De Quincey, T. (1827/2006). On murder, considered as one of the fine arts. In *The works of Thomas De Quincey: On murder, considered as one of the fine arts, revolt of the tartar*. Vol. 4. Whitefish, MT: Kessinger.

Gilmore, J. H., & Pine, B. J. (2007). *Authenticity: What consumers really want*. Cambridge, MA: Harvard Business School Press.

Keough, T. (February 20, 2017). The plausible impossibility of authentic leadership. https://www.linkedin.com/pulse/plausible-impossibility-authentic-leadership-trent-keough.

Kruse, K. (May 12, 2013). What is authentic leadership? *Forbes*. https://www.forbes.com/sites/kevinkruse/2013/05/12/what-is-authentic-leadership/#9a42131def77.

Potter, A. (2011). *The authenticity hoax: Why the "real" things we seek don't make us happy*. New York: Harper Perennial.

Stripling, J. (March 31, 2017). In Spanier case, college leadership was on trial. *Chronicle of Higher Education*. *63*(30), A17.

Willingham, R. (2014). *Authenticity: The head, heart, and soul of selling*. New York: Prentice Hall.

Part I

Core Values

ONE

Virtues, Values, and Authenticity

> My meaning simply is, that whatever I have tried to do in life, I have
> tried with all my heart to do well; that whatever I have devoted myself
> to, I have devoted myself to completely; that in great aims and in small,
> I have always been thoroughly in earnest.
> —Charles Dickens, *David Copperfield* (1850/2004) 613

Imagine this scenario: You are a department chair at a university that has a strict policy forbidding faculty members from having sexual relations with students. If faculty members violate this policy, their supervisors are advised to dismiss them (even if they're tenured), although supervisors do have a great deal of flexibility in whether or not to enforce this penalty. Specifically, the university's policies allow chairs and deans to use their best judgment about what an appropriate punishment should be in cases like this.

You have evidence that one of your faculty members did indeed have a sexual relationship with a student. But you feel uneasy about firing this faculty member because, three years ago during a very low period in your life, you yourself had an affair with a student.

For whatever reason (perhaps the student has since died or perhaps he or she was a foreign exchange student who has now returned to his or her remote village on the other side of the planet), you have every reason to believe that no one will ever learn about your indiscretion. In fact, in the time since this single lapse of judgment occurred, you've encountered no indication at all that anyone even suspected you of any misconduct.

The dean is urging you to dismiss the guilty faculty member, but you know that you'd be a hypocrite if you did so. However, despite your own actions, the policy is one that you believe in because you have witnessed several other students whose careers were harmed by such incidents even if they were willing participants in the affair at the time. You are senior enough in your position to know that, if you lost your job for any reason, finding a new position would be extremely difficult. Moreover, your spouse and children (none of whom know about your affair) would be devastated if word of it came out.

Do you fire the faculty member, assuming, "Just because I did something wrong, that doesn't excuse this faculty member's violation of this valid and important school policy. Besides, I've learned from my mistake, and I would never do it again"?

Do you tell your supervisor, "Since I'm allowed to make an exception using my own professional judgment, I'm not going to fire the faculty member this time. I don't want to ruin someone's life and career because of a single lapse in judgment"?

Do you punish someone for something that you did yourself without any punishment? How do you prioritize the values of honesty, justice, mercy, equity, and responsibility that are all involved in the situation?

When I've presented the scenario we've just considered in various leadership development workshops, the reactions of the participants have varied widely. For some, the hypocrisy of punishing someone else for something they themselves did would simply be unbearable, so they can't imagine punishing the faculty member. For others, protecting their own jobs, sparing harm to the innocent (their spouses and children), and avoiding what might happen if their deans and families found out what they did is simply an unimaginable alternative, so they can't imagine owning up to their own indiscretions. Still, for others, different issues take precedence.

In this book, we're going to explore ethical challenges like the scenario just described and consider mechanisms for discovering, not *the* answer to the questions such challenges raise, but *your* answers. And we'll come to recognize that the relationship between what we'll call authenticity and principle-based leadership is often far more complex than we may initially believe.

Your desire at this point is probably to get back to all the issues raised in our initial scenario or to start exploring others like it. But to make these reflections more meaningful, we must first lay some groundwork for our discussions of moral and ethical challenges, authentic leadership, and the difference between values and virtues. This background information may appear a bit academic at times, but I promise that it's essential if we're to understand the way through the thickets of our own ethical dilemmas.

SCANDALS, LACK OF VALUES, AND ACADEMIC LEADERSHIP

Critics of higher education have long accused professors and administrators of living in an ivory tower. The idea is that life at a college or university is far removed from the practical concerns of day-to-day life in the "real world" and that the challenges of life outside the academy rarely intrude upon the effete and theoretical environment of teaching, research, and service. But, as so often happens with stereotypes, reality has a way of challenging such a simplistic view of what takes place at most institutions of higher education.

- From 2010 through 2012, investigations at the University of North Carolina at Chapel Hill revealed that the institution allowed hundreds of student athletes to retain their eligibility to participate in intercollegiate athletics by enrolling them in courses "in which . . . [the students] didn't go to class . . . didn't have to take notes, have to stay awake . . . didn't have to meet with professors . . . didn't have to pay attention or necessarily engage with the material" and for which they were typically awarded a high grade (Lyall, 2014).
- On June 22, 2012, Pennsylvania State University football's former defensive coordinator Jerry Sandusky was found guilty of forty-five counts of sexual abuse over a fifteen year period, leading to the firing of head football coach Joe Paterno, athletic director Tim Curley, senior vice president Gary Schultz, and president Graham Spanier who, it was alleged, either knew or should have known about Sandusky's illicit behavior (Chappell, 2012). The university's official statement on this incident read, in part, "Penn State has extraordinary expectations of our leaders, who must set and maintain the example for reporting, ethics and compliance that reflect best practices. . . . [T]hese former leaders fell short" (Penn State News, 2017).
- In an article for the *Washington Post*, Daniel de Vise listed eight other scandals that cost university presidents their jobs, including the alleged affair of Hillsdale College's former president George C.

Roche III with his own daughter-in-law, the University of Illinois's use of a "clout list" that provided special consideration to applicants with political connections, and expense account abuses at American University, Montgomery College, and the University of California, Santa Cruz. In three of the scandals listed by de Vise, key players committed suicide (de Vise, 2011).

- John Diamond's book *Please Delete* (2015) describes how overspending within the University of Arkansas's office of university advancement allegedly spun out of control into a series of cover-ups, deceptions, and forced resignations.
- Stephen Trachtenberg's book *Presidencies Derailed* (2013) recounts numerous examples of sexual, financial, and interpersonal misconduct that led to the resignation or firing of university CEOs and ongoing problems for the institutions where they worked.

The sheer number of these scandals raises the question of how the moral compass of the academic leaders involved in them could have led them to such disastrous conclusions. Did the presidents, coaches, and deans at these institutions have no code of values that would have prevented these tragedies, or were they simply too preoccupied with achieving a certain end—such as success in intercollegiate athletics or protection of their school's reputation—that the means they used took precedence over any related ethical issues?

THE CALL FOR AUTHENTIC LEADERSHIP

At the beginning of the twenty-first century, similar leadership failures led Bill George, the former chairman and CEO of the medical technology company Medtronic, to call for a return to what he called **authentic leadership**.

George witnessed the collapse of companies like the energy and commodities giant Enron and the accounting firm Arthur Andersen and attributed their failures to a lack of integrity and an emphasis on profit above basic standards of acceptable moral behavior.

> We do not need executives running corporations into the ground in search of personal gain. We do not need celebrities to lead our companies. We do not need more laws. *We need new leadership.* We need authentic leaders, people of the highest integrity, committed to building enduring corporations. We need leaders who have a deep sense of

purpose and are true to their core values. (George and Sims, 2003, 9; emphasis in original)

As George's book on authentic leadership continues, he even provides a framework for the values that he believes are common to authentic leaders. George identifies what he calls five dimensions of an authentic leader that lead to five characteristics of how these leaders interact with others.

1. The leader's understanding of his or her purpose in life and in business leads to a passion for the principles that define this purpose.
2. Practicing solid values—which George says "are shaped by personal beliefs, developed through study, introspection, and consultation with others" (George, 2003, 20), but must include integrity—leads to behavior that embodies those values.
3. Leading with heart and concern for others leads to compassion, not just for those in one's inner circle, but for anyone who is struggling or facing difficult challenges.
4. Establishing connected relationships with those for whom the leader is responsible leads to trusting in and being trusted by others.
5. Demonstrating self-discipline leads to consistency, reliability, and the ability to serve as a positive role model for others. (George, 2003, 18–25 and 36–43)

Four years later, George expanded on these ideas in *True North* (2007), a book that serves as something of a sequel to *Authentic Leadership* (2003). To a certain extent, his later approach is more flexible and more responsive to the fact that different leaders may be guided by different values that arise from their own distinct experience, education, and worldviews.

[Your individual True North] is derived from your most deeply held beliefs, your values, and the principles you lead by. It is your internal compass, unique to you, that represents who you are at your deepest level. [Y]our truth is derived from your life story. As Warren Bennis said, "You are the author of your life." (George and Sims, 2007, 1)

Make no mistake about it: George is still hoping that each leader's own "unique" beliefs, values, and principles include integrity, compassion, trust, consistency, and all the other ideals recommended in *Authentic Leadership*. It is merely that *True North*, with its profiles of the forty-seven leaders George chose as exemplars, makes more explicit the author's understanding that no two people are exactly alike, and, thus, the values that inspire them are also unlikely to be exactly alike, although he assumes there will be a great deal of overlap.

The intellectual framework behind *Authentic Leadership* and *True North* owes a great deal to mid-twentieth-century existentialism, although George never mentions these philosophers, novelists, and dramatists in either book. That omission is not surprising. By the start of the twenty-first century, existentialist views had permeated Western thought in much the same way that the scent of a strong cologne, initially striking and powerful, later dissipates to the point that, even though it's still present, people aren't consciously aware of it.

It wasn't Warren Bennis but Jean-Paul Sartre, whose *Existentialism and Humanism* appeared in both French and English in 1943, who most memorably declared that people are free to define themselves however they wish, but they are then obliged to responsibility for their choices. Moreover, even before Sartre, Søren Kierkegaard had argued that a major goal in life is to be the person who one really is, and Martin Heidegger, whose influence on Sartre was profound, had drawn a sharp distinction between the roles that others impose on us and who we really are or, as we might now say, our authentic selves.

By the end of World War II and the start of the 1950s, an emphasis on authenticity was already such a commonplace in popular culture that William Whyte could decry its absence in *The Organization Man* (1956) and J. D. Salinger's protagonist Holden Caulfield could condemn those lacking it as "phonies" in *The Catcher in the Rye* (1945). (For a survey of existentialism's rise and influence on society, see Bakewell, 2016.)

Despite these philosophical underpinnings, Peter Northouse, professor emeritus of communication in the School of Communication at Western Michigan University, characterizes George's concept of authentic leadership as a *practical*, "how to" approach based on personal traits and characteristics.

He contrasts this perspective with the more theoretical approach to authentic leadership taken by authors such as William Gardner, Bruce Avolio, and Fred Walumbwa (2005), and others in their literature review of studies on authentic leadership, reports to the Gallup Leadership Institute, and subsequent studies. As Northouse notes, these authors define authentic leadership as:

a pattern of leader behavior that draws upon and promotes both positive psychological capacities and a positive ethical climate, to foster greater self-awareness, an internalized moral perspective, balanced processing of information, and relational transparency on the part of leaders working with followers, fostering positive self-development. (Walumbwa, Peterson, Avolio, Wernsing, and Gardner, 2008, 94)

He emphasizes the relationship between the leader's authenticity and his or her followers' happiness and well-being (Northouse, 2016, 201).

Northouse then identifies four positive psychological attributes (confidence, hope, optimism, and resilience) and four essential components that he regards as integral to these theoretical models:

- *Self-awareness*, the understanding of one's own strengths, weaknesses, and core values.
- *Internalized moral perspective*, the use of one's own moral compass, rather than societal pressure or a concern for appearances, to guide one's actions and decisions.
- *Balanced processing*, the ability to see matters objectively, take the perspectives of others into account, and act on an understanding of the whole picture rather than one's biases and preconceived notions.
- *Relational transparency*, the practice of being oneself rather than playing a role or adopting a façade in all situations and of speaking one's mind diplomatically but honestly with others. (Northouse, 2016, 202–4)

Or in the far more straightforward version of Ronald Riggio, the Henry R. Kravis Professor of Leadership and Organizational Psychology at Claremont McKenna College:

- Know thyself (i.e., Self-awareness);
- Do the right thing (Internalized moral perspective);
- Be fair-minded (Balanced processing);
- Be genuine (Relational transparency). (Riggio, 2014)

Taken together then, the work of Bill George and others begins to create a recognizable portrait of the kind of people whom many would regard as authentic leaders: These leaders know who they are and what they stand for, act consistently on those principles, and adhere to a set of values that place the welfare of the organization they serve and of society as a whole above narrow self-interest.

PRINCIPLES, VIRTUES, AND VALUES

Of course, the idea that leaders should be principled and transparent about who they are is hardly a product of the twenty-first century. Robert Terry (1938–2002) is one important figure whom Northouse omits in his detailed analysis of how the concept of authentic leadership developed. Terry served as senior fellow and director of the Reflective Leadership Center at the Humphrey Institute of Public Affairs at the University of Minnesota. (Northouse does, however, mention Terry briefly in another work on this topic; see Northouse, 2015, 236.)

For Terry, authentic leaders have linked their internal and external selves. They haven't deceived others about who they are, what they want, and what their goals are—and most importantly they haven't deceived themselves. There is an unbroken progression from the leaders' views of themselves and the world, to the values that arose from these views, to the actions that were based on these values, and to the conclusions about the leaders that others drew from their actions.

Those ideas will seem similar to those of the other writers on authentic leadership that we've already encountered. But one notion that distinguishes Terry from many other writers on this topic is his sharp condemnation of moral relativism.

> Relativists, who resist any claim to absolute truth, view their perspective as a safeguard against dogmatism, tyranny, and all other oppressions instituted by those who believe they have certain knowledge of the truth. Absolutists, in contrast, depict relativism as offering an intellectual haven for any abuse of power, because relativism lacks a universal ethical principle. Relativists, they argue, reduce truth to power, politics, and opinion. [For this reason, authentic leadership should be based on] our ultimate question of what is really true, believable, and trustworthy. . . . Authenticity faces the inauthentic, names it, and in hope, seeks to transform it into a new authenticity. (Terry and Cleveland, 1993, 125–26)

As a vehicle for clarifying how leaders should face inauthenticity in themselves and others and then transform it into a new authenticity, Terry developed what he called an **action wheel**, a simplified version of which appears as figure 1.1. The idea behind the action wheel is that, whenever an issue, challenge, or opportunity occurs in one of the domains on the wheel, it is best addressed by considering that domain and the one immediately clockwise from it.

For example, when an organization faces a structural challenge—recognizable, according to Terry, by the presence of complaints like "The job is not clearly defined. I don't know what I'm supposed to do," or "Our hands are so tied by red tape we can't operate"—that challenge is best addressed by taking a careful look at the organization's structure and then proceeding to the item clockwise from structure on the wheel: power and how it is allocated and exercised within the organization.

The problem, Terry senses, is that it feels more intuitive to address the issue by moving *counterclockwise*, to solve a structural challenge through *resources* by "throwing money at the problem," which rarely leads to a successful conclusion. The action wheel is thus intended to be a tool that leaders can use to guide themselves in being more effective both at diag-

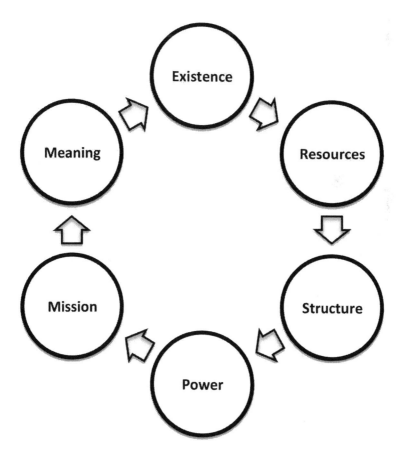

Figure 1.1. Robert Terry's Action Wheel (Simplified)

nosing issues as they arise (by assigning them to one of the six domains on the action wheel) and at addressing them (by channeling their energy on that domain and the one immediately clockwise from it).

Key to Terry's structure of the action wheel is his belief that, just as the actions of a leader must flow from his or her values, so must an organization's allocation of resources, concept of structure, and exercise of power flow from its mission, sense of meaning, and reason for existence. In this way, Terry's concept of authentic leadership becomes inextricable from what I'm going to call **principle-based**, **value-based**, or even **virtue-based leadership**. The key element of these approaches is a belief that leadership is at its most effective—or at least at its most admirable—when it is based on certain moral precepts.

For the purpose of this book, I'll refer to moral precepts of any kind as *principles*. If an author's assumption is that those moral precepts are fixed and unchanging regardless of circumstances, I'll refer to them as *virtues*. Virtues are what ethicists refer to as *deontological* in nature; that is to say, they bind us to a particular duty or course of action, regardless of consequences.

If, however, an author believes that the principles that guide the leader should be determined by the situation and perhaps even variable according to the leader's philosophy and perspective, I'll label those principles as *values*. Virtues are seen as universal, values as individual.

The difference between virtues and values goes well beyond semantics. Explicitly rejecting the situational or relativistic notion that the values of leaders are shaped by and must reflect their individual circumstances, theoretical framework, and experience, Karl Haden and Rob Jenkins argue that, in order for leadership to remain sustainable and respectable over time, leaders must live lives that embody nine specific *virtues*:

- humility;
- honesty;
- courage;
- perseverance;
- hope;
- charity;
- balance;
- wisdom;
- justice. (Haden and Jenkins, 2016, 42–64)

Those virtues, the authors argue, are unchanging and invariable, regardless of time, place, or experience.

> Virtue is at the very core of the effective leader's being. It is the foundation of moral goodness. Virtues are deeply ingrained character traits that underlie and inform everything we do, everything we say, everything we *are*. . . . Virtue . . . is the foundation of what we consider *true* ethical behavior: behavior that not only is morally correct in any given circumstance but also genuine, sincere, and consistent over time. (Haden and Jenkins, 2016, 7, 15)

Any deviation from the nine virtues Haden and Jenkins outline or any indication that other values might be more appropriate in a different time or setting would be dismissed by the authors as "flavor of the month" thinking, the notion that we're free to choose our own values based on our own life experiences (Haden and Jenkins, 2016, 5). In fact, Haden and Jenkins argue that understanding and practicing the specific virtues they identify provide an almost foolproof approach for improving one's leadership skills.

> As you come to understand, work to cultivate, and put into practice the virtues we discuss in this book, you will, over time, become a better person; as a result, we believe this means you will also become a better leader. (Haden and Jenkins, 2016, 6)

This approach, based in the belief that there are indeed specific virtues that apply to everyone everywhere and that cultivating these virtues provides the key to better leadership, can be contrasted with the one taken by Harry Kraemer, who, in *From Values to Action: The Four Principles of Values-Based Leadership* (2011), encourages leaders to identify their own values and recognize that these may be different from those of others based on circumstances, goals, and worldviews.

Unlike Haden and Jenkins's nine virtues, Kraemer's four principles are more guides to good practice than requisites to acceptable behavior. In particular, Kraemer recommends that leaders:

- Engage in self-reflection;
- Practice the sort of attentiveness that shows that the leader's own perspective aligns with that of others (an idea quite similar to Northouse's *balanced processing*);
- Act with confidence in their own abilities;

- Combine that confidence with humility about one's own weaknesses and failings. (Kraemer, 2011, 13–76)

These principles—particularly the first two—Kraemer believes, lead one to recognize the values that define who the person is and should be relied on to guide his or her action as a leader.

> To define your values, you must engage in self-reflection. Ask yourself, *What do I truly believe? Am I willing to state my values? Am I willing to compromise my values? Are my actions consistent with my beliefs?* Once you have put your values down on paper and you are clear about what you stand for, take the time to reflect more deeply by asking, *Who am I, and how comfortable am I with myself?* (Kraemer, 2011, 83)

Kraemer's last question—How comfortable am I with myself?—illustrates the degree to which a leader's reflection values sometimes begin to meld with authentic leadership. After all, if you're going to be true to yourself and your most cherished ideals, you have to know what those ideals are and how they relate to your view of the world.

That's a rather different approach from the one taken by Haden, Jenkins, and Terry who posit that it's not up to the leader to determine which values he or she is going to uphold; it is, in fact, specific virtues that determine whether or not one is a leader. As Terry says, "Our ethical principles are the final appeal, the last stop in our argument—when each of us says, in effect, 'I did it because it is right, because it is good, because it is the fitting thing to do'" (Terry and Cleveland, 1993, 68).

What Terry has termed *authentic* leadership is thus more properly regarded as *virtue-based leadership*. As we'll explore in greater detail in chapter 5, trying to affirm the importance of specific virtues at the same time as advocating for greater transparency and genuineness in leaders creates what I call the **Paradox of Authenticity**.

What happens if a leader truly doesn't believe in, for instance, Haden and Jenkins's nine virtues? In other words, what should a person do if he or she happens to be arrogant, dishonest, cowardly, uncommitted, pessimistic, greedy, self-centered, foolish, and unjust? Should that person simply give up the hope of ever being a leader or at least of being an effective leader? Or does the person have to practice virtue, as Haden and Jenkins suggest, until they actually believe what they had initially only pretended to believe? Doesn't that make them insincere, hypocritical, and inauthentic?

The point is that you can't have it both ways: Unless all leaders happen to believe in precisely the same principles (a condition that, despite what Haden and Jenkins allege, history and our own experience would argue strongly against), at least some of them have to make a choice between being authentic and adhering to whichever set of principles happens to be under consideration.

To take but one example, we can talk all we want about how admirable it would be for leaders to be humble, but there are plenty of examples of people, from Homeric heroes through at least one modern president, whom were regarded by many as exemplary leaders without the slightest hint of humility. It's not a very comfortable choice if your only options are to be either an authentic knave or a hypocritical saint or either to "fake it till you make it" (provided you ever do) or to be content in your own skin and accept yourself for the genuine rascal and reprobate that you are.

To be fair, Terry does seem to have been fully aware of this possible tension between being authentic and being virtuous, at least in terms of the figures he regarded as his own intellectual forebears. Quoting the philosopher Mike W. Martin, Terry asserts:

> [In the Authenticity Tradition,] authenticity "is defined in terms of avoiding self-deception. This emphasis leads to intensified criticism of virtually all self-deception—not just self-deception about wrongdoing—as cowardly and dishonest. . . . Existentialists, who represent the main current in the Authenticity Tradition, are preoccupied with the process of decision making. Their concern is not so much with *what* choices are made as with *how* they are made." (Terry and Cleveland, 1993, 108, quoting Martin, 1986, 53; the ellipsis is Terry's; the emphasis is Martin's)

In other words, in the Authenticity Tradition, as exemplified by Sartre and other existentialists, the one immovable virtue is authenticity. As long as a person is acting authentically in accordance with his or her core principles, no one has a right to insist that those core principles include this virtue or that value. The principles that guide me arise out of my own culture, perspective on the world, and life experience. Even if I had an identical twin, his life experience wouldn't be *exactly* the same as mine, and thus he may well believe in values that I can't support, and vice versa.

The irony that arises from this perspective is, of course, that writers within the Authenticity Tradition usually deny the universality of virtues while simultaneously declaring the universal significance of one particular virtue: authenticity itself.

PRINCIPLES AND DECISION MAKING

We seem to have come a long way from where we began, with a specific case of a hypothetical academic leader and a decision that he or she has to make. But this background on authenticity, academic leadership, principles, virtues, and values now provides us with a better understanding of the choices facing our imaginary academic leader. Armed now with these concepts, we can return to the scenario with which this chapter began and examine it in light of how different leadership approaches might guide us in making our decision.

If, for example, our leader were guided by the nine virtues advocated by Haden and Jenkins, it may seem obvious what he or she has to do. Honesty would demand that he or she take responsibility for past indiscretions. Courage would require facing the consequences for those actions, as unpleasant as they may be. Justice would insist that both the errant faculty member and the academic leader be subject to equitable sanctions.

And so, the academic leader should confess the affair with the former student to his or her family, the institution, and other relevant stakeholders, accept the formal penalties and strain in interpersonal relationships that result, and hold the faculty member to the same high standards. It all seems very clear and simple.

And yet, where the matter suddenly becomes rather less clear and simple is when we realize that other virtues among the nine selected by Haden and Jenkins might cause our academic leader to reach a very different conclusion.

Charity might cause the leader in question to recognize that even the best people make mistakes and ought to be given second chances.

Hope might inspire the person to trust that, just as his or her own past impropriety was never again repeated and was actually the cause of some personal growth, so, too, might be the case with the faculty member who has done something similar.

Wisdom might suggest that causing anguish to the academic leader's spouse and family for something that happened in the past and can't be undone is unfair to them and doesn't serve to help the current situation anyway.

Perseverance might suggest that, rather than making radical changes in the lives of many people, both the academic leader and the faculty member would do more good by making continual, steady, and determined progress to be better people in the future.

And humility might even remind the academic leader, "This situation isn't really about you. It's about what makes sense for the most people over the long term. Don't go disrupting people's lives simply because *you* feel guilty."

In other words, one of the challenges of trying to adhere to multiple virtues or values simultaneously is that they sometimes seem to contradict one another. We're torn between demonstrating justice or mercy in given situations. We value being honest, but we're likely to favor a diplomatic lie if our honesty would hurt someone's feelings without accomplishing a greater good. As a result, two factors tend to become important whenever we try to make difficult decisions based on our principles:

- The principles to which we adhere always form some sort of hierarchy. When conflicts arise between two principles, we base our decision on whichever value we regard as more important or at least more important in the given situation.
- That phrase "in the given situation" illustrates part of the weakness that comes from regarding our principles as virtues and not as values. No matter how absolute we believe any given principle must be, we inevitably interpret that "absolute" principle according to the specific situation in which we apply it. We may believe, for example, that stealing is wrong under any and all circumstances but then question the unqualified application of that principle in the case of a mother who steals a loaf of bread to feed her starving children. For any virtue we can think of, we can also think of situations in which violation of that principle should be permitted because some other overriding principle takes precedence.

Some readers might object that this second factor actually demonstrates that certain virtues are indeed absolute: Whichever principle ultimately guided our decision was, by our own admission, the most important and therefore should guide our actions in any and all circumstances.

But the fact of the matter is that we might regard the same principle as utterly significant in one situation and far less significant in another. There are times when it seems right to act on the basis of justice rather than mercy and times when it seems right to act on the basis of mercy rather than justice. There are times when we're better off acting on hope rather than wisdom and times when we're better off acting on wisdom rather than hope. Human experience is simply far too rich and complex for a "one size fits all" approach to moral principles to be an effective guide to decision making.

Nevertheless, although it's all but impossible for most people to identify any one principle that supersedes all others in guiding their actions 100 percent of the time, each of us does have a small set of principles that guides us more frequently than others. These are our **core principles**. The very fact that no two persons' sets of core principles may be identical makes it difficult to regard them as inflexible and all-encompassing virtues. And so, we may as well refer to them as people do in common parlance: **core values**.

A person's core values are certainly not his or her *only* values; they're merely the principles that tend to take precedence over other principles when there is a conflict. As such, core values can be seen as a key to character—not general human character, but the individual character of the person who holds those principles dear. They're an outgrowth of the culture in which that person grew up, combined with experience, education, reflective insight, and many other factors that affect each of us as we grow and develop.

For academic leaders, certain values also stand at our core in another way. As illustrated in figure 1.2, there are several codes that govern our actions and decisions as academic leaders:

- At the outermost layer, our behavior is guided by general principles of acceptable behavior. Neither laws nor institutional policies spell out everything that is regarded as inappropriate in civilized society, but we're expected to abide by these social norms or risk disapproval, reprimand, or sanctions for our disrespectful behavior.
- More formally, we are governed by what the law requires of everyone. Laws are based sometimes on widely accepted moral princi-

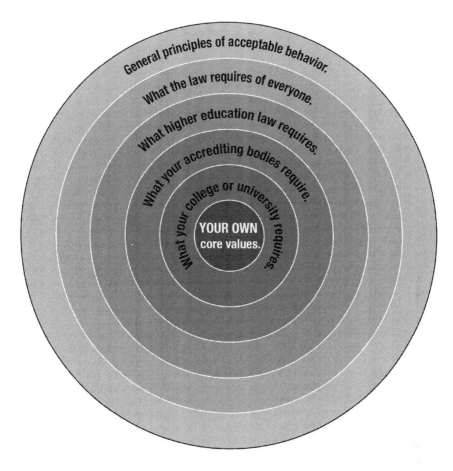

Figure 1.2. The Core Values of an Academic Leader

ples (such as prohibitions against murder, theft, and assault), sometimes on mere conventions that allow for society to function in an
orderly way (such as national laws requiring people to drive on the
left side of the road in some countries or on the right side in others),
and sometimes on principles that are regarded as moral by some
people and immoral by others (such as laws against adultery,
homosexuality, and cohabitation by unmarried members of the opposite sex).

- Beyond that, we are subject to higher education law. People who
work in other professions can safely ignore these principles, but we
can't because they're integral to what we do as leaders.

- Next, there are the policies of the various accrediting bodies that guide our actions. In addition to the standards and requirements of whichever regional accrediting body we may belong to, there may also be further rules imposed by the specialized accrediting group of any professional organization associated with a discipline we supervise.
- Even further, we have the policies and procedures of our own college and university. If you've worked at a number of different institutions, you may have observed how variable those policies and procedures can be. Sometimes what is forbidden at one institution (for example, using an institutional credit card to purchase food or drink while on a business trip) is mandatory at another. As we saw with laws in general, some of these regulations are the result of adherence to certain moral principles (such as research integrity policies), while others are mere conventions (such as the procedures for acquiring a parking permit).
- At the very center of all these codes is our own set of core values. Those values may reflect and harmonize with the other codes, exceed them in stringency or rigor, or contradict one or more of the other codes governing us. In the latter case, we face a moral or legal dilemma and may be challenged to engage in civil or institutional disobedience. For example, if we happened to work in an area where both the law and our school's own policy require us to report undocumented students to the federal authorities, but our personal set of core values included a commitment to educate any student who came to us regardless of background, we would have to choose between violating one of our core principles or suffering whatever sanctions the law and our own institution might provide.

As we'll see in the next section and then throughout succeeding chapters, this framework of successive layers of behavioral codes, with our own core values at the center, provides us with a way of understanding why authenticity is so important to the actions and decisions of academic leaders. In addition, we'll consider why authenticity and authentic leadership should be assigned special significance in our journey as academic leaders.

INTEGRITY AND AUTHENTICITY

For a decade, Robert Cipriano and Richard Riccardi of Southern Connecticut State University have been surveying academic department chairs across North America to determine their levels of experience, interests, challenges, future goals, and other aspects of their professional careers.

Over the course of their study, 98.1 percent of respondents indicated that they regarded character and integrity as necessary skills or competencies for a chair to be effective. Moreover, 80.3 percent reported that they considered them as *essential* skills or competencies for chairs (Cipriano and Riccardi, 2017, 10–13).

In this way, character and integrity, which are often viewed as closely related to authenticity, are regarded by many people as practically a prerequisite for effective leadership in higher education. (On where distinctions between integrity and authenticity can be made, see chapter 6.) Once people lose faith in your integrity, the Cipriano–Riccardi surveys suggest, all your skills in strategic planning, budgeting, decision-making, and effective communication cease to matter.

A series of studies conducted at Yale University by Jillian Jordan, Roseanna Sommers, Paul Bloom, and David Rand, give some insight into why authenticity, integrity, and character are so often assigned a privileged position in the scale of human values. They discovered that

> People tended to take someone's normative statements—such as "It is morally wrong to waste energy"—as an indication of how the speaker himself acted. In fact, our findings show that people would be more likely to believe that the speaker did not waste energy if he said, "It is wrong to waste energy," than if he simply said, "I do not waste energy." (Jordan, Sommers, and Rand, 2017, SR9)

In other words, normative statements are seen by others as a claim to virtue. When someone says, "It is morally wrong to waste energy," others interpret that statement as meaning, "I am morally right because I don't waste energy."

When those claims are later revealed to be hypocritical—that is, when the person is later exposed as inauthentic—people are simultaneously revolted at having been deceived, aware that the speaker has engaged in an admittedly immoral act, and embarrassed because they themselves may have failed to live up to the speaker's false claims of morality.

It's not simply that he fails to practice what he preaches or that he criticizes others for transgressions he, too, commits. It's that his outspoken moralizing falsely conveys his own virtue, earning him undue reputational benefits — and at the expense of the individuals whom he publicly shames. *He would be better off if he simply admitted that he sometimes falls short of these ideals himself.* (Jordan, Sommers, and Rand, 2017, SR9; emphasis added)

In short, he would have been judged less harshly had he been an authentic knave than a hypocritical saint. (For more detail on these studies and the data from which the authors draw their conclusions, see Jordan, Sommers, Bloom, and Rand, 2017.)

In academic life, we'd surely prefer our leaders to be humble, honest, brave, steadfast, and representative of all the rest of Haden and Jenkins's virtues. Too often, we're disappointed that they're not. But that disappointment doesn't begin to approach the outrage and sense of betrayal that we feel when they have held themselves up as exemplars of certain principles and insisted that we, too, aspire to those principles, only for them to be unmasked at some later point as frauds.

The legitimate power that they receive due to their positions was enhanced by the moral stature we erroneously assigned them. Once they've been revealed as dishonest claimants to the moral high ground, even the legitimate power of their position often can't compensate for the loss of ethical status they've endured. There's a reason why the nonbinding action taken by faculty members against administrators whom they view as no longer worthy of their positions is called a "vote of no confidence": The faculty has lost confidence in the ability of the administrator to act effectively on the basis of a shared set of principles and goals.

To return yet again to the hypothetical academic leader with which we began, let's imagine several scenarios and consider which would yield the least acceptable result:

a. The academic leader decides to offer a second chance to the faculty member while admitting that he or she was guilty of a similar indiscretion in the past.
b. The academic leader decides to fire the faculty member while admitting that he or she was guilty of a similar indiscretion in the past.

   c. The academic leader decides to keep his or her own past actions a secret, but to offer a second chance to the faculty member who is guilty of a similar action.

   d. The academic leader decides to keep his or her own past actions a secret, but to fire the faculty member who is guilty of a similar action.

In scenario (a), the academic leader's past provides a context that explains the reason why he or she is inclined to mercy rather than punishment in the case of the faculty member; although the academic leader may suffer institutional sanctions and long-term damage to the relationship with his or her family, there are also likely to be many who will respect the academic leader's courage and view the faculty member's penalty as just.

In scenario (b), the result may be similar although the academic leader is likely to receive even more severe institutional sanctions. If those sanctions include a salary reduction or job loss, the leader's relationship with his or her family will be further strained, perhaps irreparably.

In scenario (c), if the truth comes out later, the academic leader will be condemned as hypocritical, but at least the mercy demonstrated to the faculty member will be understood by those who may have questioned it at the time.

It is scenario (d) that seems to offer the worst possible outcome. If the truth comes out later, the sanctions imposed on the academic leader are likely to be quite severe (since the act itself was coupled with deception), the leader's relations with his or her family will be greatly damaged, his or her credibility will be utterly destroyed, and all of the other initiatives, actions, and decisions made by the leader could be called into question. People will wonder, "If she or he was deceptive to us about that, what else were we deceived about?"

The reason why the last scenario is potentially the most destructive is that the academic leader in it was the most inauthentic. From the Watergate scandal in 1972 onward, one lesson of unethical leadership has been reinforced many times: **It's often not the misdeed but the attempt to cover it up that does the most damage to reputations, institutions, and personal legacies.**

We don't always expect our academic leaders to be embodiments of virtue, but we do expect them to demonstrate integrity and authenticity. So, if we seek to become effective academic leaders, we must strive to become *authentic* academic leaders, to identify the core values that shape our character and decisions, to express to others our commitment to those core values, and then to use those core values as a guide to all our actions.

In the next chapter, we'll continue our journey toward authentic academic leadership by starting to identify that small set of principles that defines the core values of each of us and that may easily be different from other leaders, even at your own college or university.

KEY POINTS FROM CHAPTER 1

- Widely publicized scandals in higher education have brought renewed attention to the need for more principled academic leadership.
- Similar scandals in the corporate world during the late twentieth century led to a call for what became known as *authentic leadership*.
- Authentic leadership occurs when those in charge of an organization lead according to principles they truly believe in instead of focusing solely on the bottom line or establishing a public persona that doesn't reflect their actual convictions.
- For the purposes of this book, the term *virtues* will be used to refer to moral precepts that are believed to be universal, applying to all people at all times in all places. The term *values* will be used to refer to moral precepts that arise from an individual's own culture and personal experience, but that may not be universally shared. The term *principles* will be used as a collective expression to refer to both virtues and values.
- Because a person's principles can sometimes come into conflict with one another, each of us has a set of core values that helps define who we are as unique individuals. These core values tend to take precedence over other principles whenever there is a conflict.
- We may then refine our notion of what an authentic leader is as a person who leads in transparent accordance with his or her core values.
- While authenticity may itself be regarded as merely another value, it assumes prominence among other values for leaders because hypocrisy—the absence of integrity or authenticity—irreparably undermines the leader's ability to exercise other values or virtues.

- Authenticity and integrity are often regarded by academic leaders themselves as particularly important, and thus authentic academic leadership can provide a useful roadmap for developing effective leadership in higher education.

REFERENCES

Bakewell, S. (2016). *At the existentialist café: Freedom, being, and apricot cocktails with Jean-Paul Sartre, Simone de Beauvoir, Albert Camus, Martin Heidegger, Karl Jaspers, Edmund Husserl, Maurice Merleau-Ponty and others.* New York: Other Press.

Chappell, B. (June 21, 2012). Penn State abuse scandal: A guide and timeline. http://www.npr.org/2011/11/08/142111804/penn-state-abuse-scandal-a-guide-and-timeline.

Cipriano, R. E., & Riccardi, R. L. (Summer 2017). Department chairs: A ten-year study. *The Department Chair. 28*(1), 10–13.

de Vise, Daniel. (November 21, 2011). Eight scandals that ended college presidencies. *Washington Post.* https://www.washingtonpost.com/blogs/college-inc/post/eight-scandals-that-ended-college-presidencies/2011/11/21/gIQA4diYiN_blog.html?utm_term=.4488fb90b559#comments.

Diamond, J. N. (2015). *Please delete: How leadership hubris ignited a scandal and tarnished a university.* Woolwich, ME: John Diamond Books.

Dickens, C. (1850/2004). *David Copperfield.* New York: Penguin.

Gardner, W. L., Avolio, B. J., & Walumbwa, F. O. (2005). *Authentic leadership theory and practice: Origins, effects and development.* Amsterdam, Netherlands: Elsevier.

George, B. (2003). *Authentic leadership: Rediscovering the secrets to creating lasting value.* San Francisco: Jossey-Bass.

George, B., & Sims, P. (2007). *True north: Discover your authentic leadership.* San Francisco: Jossey-Bass.

Haden, N. K., & Jenkins, R. (2016). *The 9 virtues of exceptional leaders: Unlocking your leadership potential.* 2nd ed. Atlanta: Deeds.

Jordan, J. J., Sommers, R., Bloom, P., & Rand, D. G. (January 20, 2017). Why do we hate hypocrites? Evidence for a theory of false signaling. *Psychological Science.* 1, (20170120): 095679761668577. Available online at https://papers.ssrn.com/sol3/papers.cfm?abstract_id=2897313.

Jordan, J. J., Sommers, R., & Rand, D. G. (January 15, 2017). The real problem with hypocrisy. *New York Times.* SR9.

Kraemer, H. M. J. (2011). *From values to action: The four principles of values-based leadership.* San Francisco: Jossey-Bass.

Lyall, S. (October 22, 2014). U.N.C. investigation reveals athletes took fake classes. *New York Times.* https://www.nytimes.com/2014/10/23/sports/university-of-north-carolina-investigation-reveals-shadow-curriculum-to-help-athletes.html.

Martin, M. W. (1986). *Self-deception and morality.* Lawrence, KS: University Press of Kansas.

Northouse, P. G. (2015). *Introduction to leadership: Concepts and practice.* 3rd ed. Los Angeles: Sage.

Northouse, P. G. (2016). *Leadership: Theory and practice.* 7th ed. Los Angeles: Sage.

Penn State News. (March 24, 2017). University comment on Spanier trial decision. http://news.psu.edu/story/458167/2017/03/24/university-comment-spanier-trial-decision.

Riggio, R. E. (January 22, 2014). What is authentic leadership? Do you have it? *Psychology Today*. https://www.psychologytoday.com/blog/cutting-edge-leadership/2014 01/what-is-authentic-leadership-do-you-have-it.

Salinger, J. D. (1945). *The catcher in the rye*. Boston: Little Brown & Co.

Sartre, J.-P. (1943). *Existentialism and humanism*. London: Methuen.

Sartre, J.-P. (1943). *L'existentialisme est un humanisme*. Paris: Nagel.

Terry, R. W., & Cleveland, H. (1993). *Authentic leadership: Courage in action*. San Francisco: Jossey-Bass Publishers.

Trachtenberg, S. J. (2013). *Presidencies derailed: Why university leaders fail and how to prevent it*. Baltimore: The Johns Hopkins University Press.

Walumbwa, F. O., Peterson, S. J., Avolio, B. J., Wernsing, T. S., & Gardner, W. L. (February, 2008). Authentic leadership: Development and validation of a theory-based measure. *Journal of Management*. 34(1), 89–126.

Whyte, W. H. (1956). *The organization man*. New York: Simon and Schuster.

RESOURCES

Blekkingh, B. W. (2015). *Authentic leadership: Discover and live your essential mission*. Oxford, UK: Infinite Ideas.

Kraemer, H. M. J. (2015). *Becoming the best: Build a world-class organization through values-based leadership*. Hoboken, NJ: Wiley.

Kuczmarski, S. S., & Kuczmarski, T. D. (1995). *Values-based leadership*. Englewood Cliffs, NJ: Prentice Hall.

Ladkin, D. (2015). *Mastering the ethical dimension of organizations: A self-reflective guide to developing ethical astuteness*. Cheltenham, UK: Edward Elgar.

Ladkin, D., & Spiller, C. (2013). *Authentic leadership: Clashes, convergences and coalescences*. Cheltenham, UK: Edward Elgar.

Lennick, D., & Kiel, F. (2011). *Moral intelligence 2.0: Enhancing business performance and leadership success in turbulent times*. Upper Saddle River, NJ: Prentice Hall.

Seligman, M. E. P. (2004). *Authentic happiness: Using the new positive psychology to realize your potential for lasting fulfillment*. New York: Free Press.

Seligman, M. E. P. (2011). *Flourish: A visionary new understanding of happiness and well-being*. New York: Free Press.

Shugart, S. (2013). *Leadership in the crucible of work: Discovering the interior life of an authentic leader*. Maitland, FL: Florida Hospital Publishing.

Starratt, R. J. (2004). *Ethical leadership*. San Francisco: Jossey-Bass.

TWO

Identifying Your Core Values

L'hypocrisie est un hommage que le vice rend à la vertu. (Hypocrisy is the compliment that vice pays to virtue.)
— François de La Rochefoucauld, *Reflections*, Maxim 218

If, as we saw in the last chapter, authenticity means being true to our core values and reflecting those values in both word and deed, then we have to know what our core values are. That's actually a more difficult task than it may initially appear.

We rarely think of our values in hierarchical terms, admitting that one value will take precedence over another when they come into conflict. Identifying that minute subset of two, three, or four values that we prize more than anything else often requires reflecting on specific circumstances and recalling situations in which we really did have to choose between competing principles.

But if we're to adopt an approach toward academic leadership that's truly authentic, we need to engage in that challenging work of sorting through the principles that motivate us and recognizing those that most define who we are as professionals and as people. In this chapter, we'll begin the process of burrowing down into our convictions and discovering which values continually motivate us, which values are important to us in certain situations but not in others, and which values we may honor more in the breach than in observance.

PRODUCT, PROCESS, AND PRINCIPLE

Among the various motivations we may have for any action, we may be focused primarily on the product or end result of what we do, the process or the action itself, or the principle or the conviction that inspires the action. Any of these motivations may well lead us to a satisfying conclusion.

In recent years, for instance, a great deal of attention in leadership and management studies has been on **product-oriented motivation**. For example, in Stephen Covey's best-selling work *The Seven Habits of Highly Effective People* (1989), the second habit—and, in my experience, the only habit that most people who have read the book tend to remember—is "Begin with the end in mind" (Covey, 1989, 99–144). In common parlance, "Keep your eyes on the prize." Remember your goal throughout the process.

That's not merely hard-headed corporate advice to remain focused on the bottom line of increasing shareholder value. We have to remember that Covey's work arises out of the same values-based tradition as the other works that we examined in chapter 1. Its subtitle is *Restoring the Character Ethic*. So, it's perfectly possible for a leader to be motivated out of concern for the end result or product and still remain ethical. That, in fact, was one of Covey's primary aims.

PRODUCT-ORIENTED MOTIVATION

In fact, one of the most influential management theories of the second half of the twentieth century was Robert House's **Path-Goal Theory**, which is all about identifying the proper goal or product and then helping subordinates in the organization determine the appropriate path to achieving it (House and Mitchell, 1974). In House's later elaboration of the theory, leaders adopt one of four management styles according to the needs and expectations of their subordinates and the circumstances surrounding current challenges or opportunities:

- *Directive* leaders tell their followers what to do. A directive leadership style is most helpful when people need more guidance to avoid uncertainty in how to handle the situation and solve problems that may arise along the way.

- *Achievement-oriented* leaders identify the goal, but have confidence in their followers to know the best ways of achieving it. Achievement-oriented leadership is most effective in professional environments where followers are highly trained and have the right level of knowledge and experience to pursue a goal without constant supervision.
- *Participative* leaders consult with their followers and incorporate their advice into determining the best pathway toward a goal. This approach, which bears many similarities to the consultative style of decision making, is most effective when people are highly trained and engaged in, or self-motivated about, their work.
- *Supportive* leaders place primary emphasis on their followers' well-being. A supportive style of leadership seeks to reduce employee stress and frustration in the workplace. Supportive leaders try to make work as pleasant as possible for others by showing concern for them and by being friendly and approachable. (House, 1996)

Even though several of these leadership styles place confidence in followers or include concern for their welfare, the ultimate aim of the Path-Goal Theory is attainment of the goal. Subordinates are merely vehicles used to reach that goal. Regardless of how participative or supportive leaders may be, if they don't accomplish the task in question, they've failed at their primary responsibility. In this way, despite the differences in names among House's four leadership styles, they are all ultimately achievement-oriented in their fundamental foci.

In higher education, we encounter product-oriented motivation in such common practices as strategic planning, performance-based funding, outcomes assessment, and the use of metrics to indicate whether a goal has been attained. The value of these practices is that they encourage us to ask ourselves regularly what it is that we're trying to accomplish at our institutions and in our programs. Rather than allowing us to become distracted by our own individual efforts to advance our careers or indulge our curiosity for its own sake, product-oriented activities direct our attention to the goal and try to unite the academic community in a common purpose.

The drawback to these approaches is that they *do* discourage academic professionals from indulging their curiosity for its own sake, even when the results of that curiosity may be benefits that are greater than the goals the institution has set.

After all, general research and reflection sometimes produces results that no one could have anticipated and thus that couldn't have been established in advance as ultimate goals. Moreover, just as we can only set a goal if we're aware of its possibility, so do many product-oriented practices in higher education cause us to pursue, not necessarily the most important goals, but the most attainable ones.

We assess the assessable and measure the measurable because evaluating progress toward goals like improving our students' leadership abilities, creativity, and ethical behavior eludes us. We settle for pursuing increases in student credit-hour production, six-year graduation rates, and the percentages of alumni employed within a year of graduation because those products are quantifiable. That's not to say that they're not important, but they do limit many people's perspectives on the benefits that a college education can provide.

THOUGHT EXPERIMENT: PRESIDENT GRIT

With these considerations in mind, let's engage in a brief thought experiment. Let's imagine that we've encountered an institution that, several years ago, hired a new chief executive officer, a person whom we'll call President Grit.

President Grit is a generally good person. He has a pleasant interpersonal style, treats others with respect, and genuinely cares about the quality of higher education. He is still relatively new to the presidency at Great Plains Commonwealth University (GPCU). He previously served as the vice president for development at Research Intensive University, a very different type of institution that is located in a region with numerous large industries and several prominent research institutes.

President Grit came to GPCU with the express intention of bringing the university to a new level of prominence. Until now, GPCU had served mostly first-generation students who grew up within a hundred miles of the university. There are very few residence halls on campus, and 87 percent of the student body commutes either from home or from apartments in Great Plains. GPCU is not the state's flagship university; in fact, no one (except perhaps its most loyal alumni) would consider it in the top tier of the state's several dozen colleges and universities.

In order to bring about the improved institutional reputation that he desires, President Grit has three main strategic goals:

- to change the university's mission from being a modestly successful teaching institution to being a cutting-edge research institution;
- to institute intercollegiate athletics, primarily basketball and hockey, the two most popular sports at Research Intensive University;
- to develop a major online education program which, until now, has been virtually nonexistent at the university.

While faculty members and students had initially been receptive to President Grit's ideas, he now faces growing apathy toward the idea of actually changing the institution's culture.

Since no current infrastructure for advanced research exists at GPCU, there is grumbling about shifting resources toward these new priorities. Since the institution has such an extensive commuter student population, those who remain on campus for athletic events are relatively few. Since most of the faculty has no experience in online education, there is reluctance to adapt courses to an unfamiliar format for a platform already well established at the state's other colleges and universities.

Imagine now that several years have passed, and President Grit is feeling frustrated that he has made so little progress on what he regards as the initiatives he has staked his reputation on. If President Grit were so goal-oriented that his desire to achieve his three strategic goals caused him to lose sight of his core principles, how might he start acting on the belief that the end justifies the means? What might he do that could harm the institution, his career, or his ability to be successful in achieving his goals?

The thought experiment is this: If you were President Grit and you wanted to be sure you avoided becoming so preoccupied with your goal that you cut corners and acted in a way that violated your principles, what might you do?

When I conduct this thought experiment in workshops, a common approach that participants try to take is to go back into the past and say that Great Plains Commonwealth University was wrong for hiring a president with a vision so different from its past successes or that President Grit was wrong for accepting a job where his vision would be so inappropriate to the school's mission.

Either or both of those notions may be correct, but they're really irrelevant to the task at hand. It's not at all uncommon for colleges and universities to hire academic leaders who, for whatever reason, prove to be imperfect fits with the mission and values of the programs they're hired to supervise. The real issue is, if you're an academic leader who ends up having an objective that your institution seems unwilling or unable to meet, what do you do?

In the scenario as it is written, we're asked to consider what might go wrong if President Grit becomes so preoccupied with achieving the goals he believes to be important that he begins to believe that the end might justify the means and thus compromise the principles that otherwise motivate him as a leader. And that's precisely the challenge that can arise for academic leaders who adopt a product-oriented motivation too exclusively.

If we become so preoccupied with graduation rates or standardized test scores—or, as in the thought experiment, changing a teaching-focused institution into a research university, promoting intercollegiate athletics because they were important to the culture of our previous school, and advancing online education because we believe our school has fallen behind this important trend—we may end up pursuing those goals at the expense of other ideals we have such as the importance of student-centeredness or our commitment to shared governance.

In President Grit's case, preoccupation with his visionary goals can be harmful to the institution because it might lose enrollment and external funding if it's seen as abandoning its traditional mission, damaging to his career if he fails in helping GPCU flourish, and counterproductive to his goals if his stubborn pursuit of them in the face of widespread opposition causes him to alienate the very people who would be necessary for their success.

Make no mistake about it: A product orientation is important in higher education as it is in many other types of organizations. If we pay no attention to what we're trying to accomplish, our programs and institutions may end up accomplishing very little. But a fixation on goals that causes us to ignore both process and principle is likely to be at least as destructive as having no goals at all.

PROCESS-ORIENTED MOTIVATION

A process-oriented motivation in leadership occurs when those who are in charge focus their attention not so much on the goals or products of an organization's activities but on the activities themselves. Process-oriented leaders tend to be very interested in policies and procedures. They want to make sure that the organization runs smoothly and efficiently, and they spend a great deal of time perfecting the organization's systems, methods, and techniques so that everyone knows precisely what to do, when to do it, and why it needs to be done.

Process-oriented leaders also spend more time working with subordinates or followers than do product-oriented leaders since it will be the subordinates or followers who play the most important role in implementing the procedures that are established. In a famous work that helped define much of management philosophy for the 1960s and 1970s, Douglas McGregor, who taught at MIT and was a former president of Antioch College, concluded that leaders pursued one of two major theories when it came to how they engaged employees in the central processes of an enterprise (McGregor, 1960).

Theory X leaders believed that people are inherently lazy, passive, and resistant to change. Employees, in the eyes of these leaders, possessed relatively little ambition and preferred to be told what to do by strong, directive leaders. Theory X managers thus tended to use threats and punishments to coerce employees to follow policies and procedures. To Theory X leaders, micromanagement was all but essential to a successful business. If leaders eased up on the pressure and tried to give employees more freedom, the work wouldn't get done and proper procedures wouldn't be followed.

The second type of leaders, **Theory Y** leaders, believed that people are inherently motivated, active, interested in doing good work, and interested in positive change. Theory Y leaders preferred to empower employees who often had their own ideas about which processes should be implemented in the organization, and those ideas tended to be better than those of many leaders since the employees worked actively with the processes themselves whereas the managers were further removed from the shop floor.

Theory Y leaders believed in open communication between labor and management. They used rewards to recognize good work, not merely punishments to sanction poor work. Under Theory Y leaders, the needs of the organization and the tasks that workers performed were better aligned, and McGregor regarded the Theory Y manager as the leader of the future, one who was better suited to the industrial and post-industrial demands of the second half of the twentieth century.

McGregor's two theories continued to have a great deal of influence on American corporate thinking until a series of recessions rocked the economies of western nations in the late 1970s and early 1980s. High rates of inflation throughout the 1970s led the chairman of the Federal Reserve, Paul Volcker, to raise interest rates, leading to a slight recession.

After a short period of recovery, the recession then returned and grew even deeper when the Iranian Revolution of 1979 created a spike in oil prices and a worldwide energy crisis. Volcker's tight money policy exacerbated the situation, and many in the west believed that the economic boom that had occurred following World War II had finally run its course. In the east, the Japanese economy was faring far better, and western managers sought to learn from their Japanese counterparts how to improve their manufacturing processes and increase the quality of their products.

Within this context, William Ouchi, a professor in the Anderson School of Management at the University of California–Los Angeles (UCLA), published *Theory Z: How American Business Can Meet the Japanese Challenge* (1981) and proposed an alternative to the McGregor model. According to Ouchi, another type of supervisor, whom he called the **Theory Z** leader, promoted the loyalty of his or her employees to an organization by taking a general interest in the employees' welfare both at work and at home.

These leaders evaluated the performance of their workers not just on quantitative measures (how much they produced, a product-oriented perspective), but also on qualitative measures (how well they worked, progressed in their jobs, and interacted constructively with colleagues, a process-oriented perspective).

In a Theory Z environment such as the *quality circles* that were common in Japanese companies, labor and management worked together to make as many decisions as possible collectively. The insights of workers were genuinely respected not merely given lip service (as tended to occur even under Theory Y leaders).

What Ouchi demonstrated, even though he never expressed it in these terms, was that, despite all the supposed emphasis on process in McGregor's Theory X and Theory Y approaches, both types of leaders were still ultimately product-oriented in their perspectives. No matter whether they trusted workers or felt obliged to coerce them to do their tasks, they still regarded workers primarily as means to the ends of the organizations' primary products.

Only in a Theory Z system was process truly given the attention it deserved. Workers were actually given the authority they needed to make decisions about improvement of processes. If the workers' attention was expected to be on the final results or products, the managers' attention was expected to be on the workers.

In higher education, Theory Z approaches tend to occur when administrators adopt what I've elsewhere referred to as **organic academic leadership** (Buller, 2015, 217–39). In organic academic leadership, the goal is not as much to establish and implement a vision as it is to create an environment in which faculty members and students thrive.

It is organic because it adopts an environmental, even agricultural model for the leader's primary task. Just as a gardener helps plants to bear fruit not by trying to urge or pressure them toward fruitfulness, but by creating a rich environment in which they can grow, so does the organic academic leader see his or her job as making sure that the institution's stakeholders are well cared for and have what they need in order to bear the fruits of insight, understanding, and original discovery.

Like other process-oriented leadership approaches, organic academic leadership recognizes that there's a paradox to the product-oriented approach. By being preoccupied with the end product, leaders often stifle the ability of others to produce that product. As illogical as it may seem, the best way to increase the quality and quantity of an organization's product is to focus not on the product itself but on the process that creates it.

PRINCIPLE-ORIENTED MOTIVATION

Principle-oriented leadership functions in a very different way from the other two types of motivation that we've considered. An emphasis on either product or process entails what we might call an **"End-Pulling" Leadership Approach**. In order to achieve some goal or improve some process, the leader is pulled along a particular path. The objective, as House suggests in his Path-Goal Theory, is to get to a certain destination as efficiently as possible.

Principle-based leadership, on the other hand, constitutes what we might call a **"Foundation-Pushing" Leadership Approach**. Instead of being drawn along a path as a way of reaching some destination, leaders are pushed in a particular direction because of their values.

For example, an academic leader who adopts a principle-oriented motivation might say something like, "Because I believe in the value that students always come first in higher education, I:

- "never take any action that puts myself, my faculty, or my program ahead of what's best for students";
- "maximize my availability to students by having a large number of office hours, getting to class early, and remaining after class whenever possible";
- "never forget that, although I am a faculty leader, I am an educator first";
- "give priority to funding projects that increase student success, even if doing so increases faculty workload or decreases funding for faculty research and travel";
- "judge each student on his or her own merits rather than prejudging students based on earlier disappointments or bad experiences."

Those actions are chosen by the academic leader not because they'll result in some product (such as increased student credit-hour production) or improve some process (such as more efficient degree audits), but because the speaker believes that they are the right things to do.

The scandals that we considered in chapter 1 didn't occur because leaders didn't identify a clear product or understand the process needed to produce that product. In fact, it is often the case that being motivated by either product or process is precisely what causes leadership failures.

Sometimes, when we become preoccupied with achieving a goal, we stop caring about the means we use to reach that goal. Sometimes, too, when our attention is absorbed by a process, we stop caring about whether that process is harming people more than it helps them.

In the public outcries that followed the University of North Carolina (UNC) Chapel Hill "paper courses" scandal or the collapse of Enron, it wasn't six-year graduation rates, a rise in shareholder value, or uniform practices of outcomes assessment that were the focus of concern. It was the fact that product and process became more important than principle.

Authenticity is also a function of attention to principle far more than product or process. Knowing the principles that motivate you is what causes you to feel inauthentic ("I'm sorry I said that. I just wasn't being myself yesterday. Those remarks don't reflect who I really am.") or authentic ("I'm proud for standing up to him. I felt like I was finally able to be the real me at work."). The problem, as we saw in chapter 1, is that each of us subscribes to a fairly large set of principles, and it's difficult to adhere to every principle in every action we take.

Sometimes we have to choose between competing principles (such as our commitment to preserve the confidence of someone who entrusted a secret to us and our commitment to help others who could only be protected if we broke that confidence) and sometimes we believe that a principle is generally a good thing to do even though we often deviate from that principle because our commitment to it is not particularly strong.

Those weaker principles or the ones we often set aside in favor of other, seemingly more pressing ethical standards aren't our main concern in trying to determine our authentic leadership style. The values that truly define us are the principles that we'd readily "go to the wall" for or, if that seems too extreme, that we'd be willing to put our jobs in jeopardy for.

These core values define who we are not just as academic leaders but as human beings. They reflect what we care about most, and they are what protect us from pursuing products that we will later regret producing and engaging in processes that may be efficient and economical but end up distracting us from the things we truly care about.

METHODS OF IDENTIFYING CORE VALUES

Our goal, therefore, should be to identify that small subset of values that truly define us as leaders and as people. But how do you do that? Fortunately, there are a number of strategies that can assist us in this process. Throughout this book, we'll explore some of the most important of these strategies. For the purposes of this chapter, however, we'll focus on what are probably the two most basic or fundamental approaches, both based on introspection and reflection.

The first strategy that we'll consider consists of completing online inventories that present the reader with a series of questions or situations, have the reader choose from a list of multiple choice responses, and then tally the results into a list of the values that the reader appears to embrace most strongly.

Among the best of these online inventories can be found in the Questionnaire Center of the University of Pennsylvania's Authentic Happiness Project (University of Pennsylvania: Authentic Happiness Questionnaire Center, 2017). Although the inventories found on the site deal with a wide range of issues related to authentic happiness and satisfaction with life, several deal specifically with core values:

- The Values in Action (VIA) Survey of Character Strengths is a list of 240 statements such as "I never quit a task before it is done" and "I always keep my promises." Participants respond to each item using a five-choice scale ranging from "Very Much Like Me" to "Very Much Unlike Me." After responding to each item, the Web site automatically ranks the priorities that the participant appears to give various concepts and ranks his or her level of commitment to twenty-four qualities such as forgiveness and mercy, humor and playfulness, and hope, optimism, and future-mindedness. The Web site refers to the qualities being ranked as *signature strengths*, and they do combine both commonly recognized ethical principles (such as kindness and generosity) with what we might consider to be character traits or preferences (such as leadership and love of learning). Nevertheless, the inventory is so thorough and has been so extensively validated that it provides a far more reliable assessment of the participant's commitment to the twenty-four qualities it surveys than do nearly all the very brief inventories on Web sites sponsored by popular magazines. For our purposes, it is interesting to note that one of the qualities ranked by the survey is the participant's commitment to honesty, authenticity, and genuineness.
- The Brief Strengths Test is a more concise version of the VIA Survey of Character Strengths.
- The VIA Strengths Survey for Children is a modified version of the character strengths survey intended for young people.
- The Transgression Motivation Questionnaire deals specifically with the participant's commitment to the value of forgiveness.
- The Gratitude Survey focuses on the degree to which the participant feels and expresses appreciation of others.
- The Grit Survey rates the participant's commitment to the value of perseverance.

- The Compassionate Love Survey "[m]easures your tendency to support, help, and understand other people." (University of Pennsylvania: Authentic Happiness Questionnaire Center, 2017)

By completing these inventories and examining the results, we can get a fairly good impression of what a set of widely used and validated instruments concludes are the principles to which we have the strongest commitment. The problem with these online inventories is that, while they are thorough, they are also extremely time-consuming, and time is the one resource that busy academic leaders have in fairly low abundance.

So, the second strategy that we'll consider can be completed in less time although it presumes that the participant already has a high level of self-awareness. With this method, the participant merely scans a list of principles and identifies those with which he or she feels a particularly close affinity. Alternatively, the participant can scan a list of vices and identify those to which he or she feels the greatest antipathy; the assumption then is that whatever value is the opposite of that vice must be one that the person cares a great deal about.

Among the most useful lists of these values and vices are the following:

- The *Personal Values Card Sort* (2001) is an exercise developed by W. R. Miller, J. C'de Baca, D. B. Matthews, and P. L. Wilbourne at the University of New Mexico. Depending on the version used, it consists of fifty to eighty-three values, each of which has its name and definition printed on a separate card. Sample values and definitions in the *Personal Values Card Sort* are "Justice: to promote fair and equal treatment for all," "Moderation: to avoid excesses and find a middle ground," and "Rationality: to be guided by reason and logic." The participant is to prepare five stacks: Least Important, Not Very Important, Neither Important nor Unimportant, Somewhat Important, and Most Important. The cards are shuffled and assigned to the different stacks, with the only rule that no stack can contain more than 10 cards. (If all eighty-three cards are used, some will have to be discarded as not even reaching the level of being Least Important. The assumption, therefore, is that all the values left in the stacks have at least *some* importance to the participant.) There are also two blank cards that the participant can fill in if he or she wishes to identify a principle not included in the standard set. When the stacks are complete, the participant then takes the cards in the Most Important stack and sorts them into priority order. The result should thus be a set of no more than ten values that the participant regards as particularly significant, with the topmost card being the one value that he or she finds most central to his or her character.

- Rhona Berens (n.d.) of Forté Dreams Coaching has assembled a list of 374 values, listed in alphabetical order from abundance to zeal. Although the values in Berens's list are not defined, readers can skim it, extracting a small subset that they believe have special importance for them.
- The *Life Values Inventory* by Duane Brown and R. Kelly Crace (1996) is a list of forty-two statements, each of which participants respond to by placing it in one of these categories: Almost Never Guides My Behavior, Sometimes Guides My Behavior, or Always Guides My Behavior. There are also two additional, unnamed categories that fall between the three named categories. Using a key that is provided, the participant then tallies his or her responses to groups of three questions, resulting in fourteen composite scores. These composite scores then indicate the importance to which the participant assigns such values as creativity ("It is important to have new ideas or to create new things"), privacy ("It is important to have time alone"), and responsibility ("It is important to be dependable and trustworthy").
- The *Personal Values Inventory*, developed by the Australian consulting firm UQ Power (2014), contains 121 words and phrases such as *experience, wordsmith,* and *lack of pretense*. The reader is first directed to choose the ten most important words or phrases on that list and then to narrow his or her choices further until there are only five. Finally, the participant is asked to identify a specific action that he or she could take in order to better embody the values that he or she has identified as most important.
- The *Huge List of Vices* by Writeworld (n.d.) is sort of a photographic negative of Rhona Berens's long list of virtues, identifying and defining 146 character flaws, including infidelity ("unfaithfulness or disloyalty, especially to a sexual partner"), grumpiness ("a fussy and eccentric disposition; bad-tempered or sullen"), and vainglory

("excessive pride in or boastfulness about personal abilities or achievements"). After scanning the list, the reader can identify a short subset of vices that he or she finds particularly troubling or difficult to forgive.

In all of these approaches, the importance of defining one's terms becomes clear as soon as a person tries to compare his or her own responses with those of someone else. For example, we saw that Brown and Crace's *Life Values Inventory* defined *privacy* as the importance of having time alone.

That, of course, is far from the only definition that word might have. To another person, privacy might consist of giving respect to someone else's idiosyncrasies or right to be alone, freedom from intrusion by the observation and judgment of others, or even the legal protection afforded to individuals by the U.S. Constitution to be free from the interference of others in their personal decision making.

THOUGHT EXPERIMENT: A FIRST ATTEMPT AT IDENTIFYING CORE VALUES

As an initial exercise in identifying your own personal core values, I have created three tables, based in part on the inventories and lists mentioned above and in part on the values and vices that participants have repeatedly identified in the workshops on authentic academic leadership I've conducted over the years:

- Table 2.1 is a list of seventy-five general virtues, values, or principles.
- Table 2.2 is a list of forty general vices, character flaws, or negative traits.
- Table 2.3 is a list of thirty-five virtues, values, or principles commonly discussed and regarded as important in higher education.

As an initial effort in trying to identify a select set of principles that you regard as your core values, conduct the following thought experiment. Go through the three tables just listed and identify the five general virtues, values, or principles that you regard as most significant; the five general vices, character flaws, or negative traits that you regard as most reprehensible; and the four higher education values or principles that you believe are most central to your motivation.

Then, once you've identified the five vices, character flaws, or negative traits that have made your short list for this exercise, see if you can identify the opposing value to each vice. For example, if arrogance is a character trait that particularly disturbs you, you might identify humility as the value that most completely opposes it.

Table 2.1.   General Virtues, Values, and Principles

Read over the list of positive qualities, and select five (and only five) that resonate with you more than others. Please note that the list is not intended to be exhaustive. To the contrary, it has been pared down in such a way to avoid as much duplication and overlap as possible. For example, rather than treating **consistency** *and* **dependability** *as two separate qualities, they are intentionally conjoined in this list because, in common usage, they often refer to very similar behaviors. For this reason, if you don't find a value on this list that you expect to see, try looking for a synonym or close alternative.*

accuracy	a commitment to getting matters right, even at the level of minor details
adaptability	the capacity to be versatile as circumstances change
altruism	the willingness to put the needs of others ahead of one's own needs
ambition	the desire to get ahead in the world and the willingness to work toward that end
assertiveness	a willingness to stand up for one's own interests
boldness	a tendency to act in a courageous and decisive manner
brilliance	a high degree of intelligence, insight, and creativity
candor	the tendency to say precisely what one means, be transparent, and act without any hidden agendas
charisma	an almost indefinable attraction that draws others to one and makes them like or admire one
cleanliness	the habit of maintaining good hygiene for oneself and one's environment
compassion	the ability to share, understand, and appreciate the feelings of others
composure	grace under pressure
confidence	the ability to act with self-assurance or poise
conviction	a tendency to let one's principles guide one's actions
cooperation	a tendency to compromise for the sake of preserving harmony
courage	bravery in situations that may cause fear in others
courtesy	acting with good manners; behaving in a way that does not make others feel uncomfortable

decisiveness	the tendency to act without hesitancy, vacillation, or regret
dependability	a certain consistency of behavior that others can count on
dignity	an accurate and not inflated understanding of one's own worth
diligence	a willingness to work hard and consistently
discretion	keeping confidence with the information entrusted to one
effectiveness	achieving goals that have been set
efficiency	achieving goals that have been set with as little expenditure of resources as possible
elegance	a sense of style and grace
eloquence	the capacity to speak effectively and with a polished style
enthusiasm	acting with spirit and gusto
expertise	a high level of knowledge and proficiency in a given area
faith	commitment to beliefs that cannot be proven by experience or reasoning
family values	a commitment to the importance of marriage, children, and wholesome activities
fitness	maintaining a state of robust physical health
friendship	support for and commitment to one's friends
gallantry	a high degree of courtesy, politeness, and thoughtfulness
generosity	a willingness to share liberally with others
gratitude	a willingness to express appreciation for the efforts of others
gregariousness	the extroverted delight in groups and group activities; a personal sense of warmth and charm that puts others at ease
honor	a commitment to protecting one's reputation by acting morally and righteously
humility	modesty; a tendency to act without pretension
ingenuity	clever creativity
integrity	a commitment to guiding one's behavior with honesty, reliability, and other positive values
intelligence	the innate capacity to learn and understand
justice	a commitment to fairness and equity
leadership	the process of influencing a group of people to move in a common direction toward a (frequently visionary) goal
learnedness	a high level of education produced by extended study
loyalty	fidelity to an idea, person, or organization
mindfulness	nonjudgmental awareness of experience as it occurs

neatness	a sense of order and a belief that everything has its proper place
open-mindedness	a willingness to consider ideas and beliefs that one does not currently share
optimism	maintaining a high level of hope in future good outcomes
originality	a capacity for novelty and creativity
passion	deep commitment, caring, and emotional investment
patriotism	love of one's country, its achievements, and its values
perseverance	the tendency to stick with an activity for an extended period and not give up easily
practicality	the habit of being realistic and not caught up in unreasonable dreams or impossible goals
professionalism	acting in a manner that is expected in the business world or other professional settings
punctuality	a tendency to be on time and to complete one's work on time
refinement	acting in a polished, cultured, and sophisticated manner
self-control	keeping one's behavior and emotions in check despite provocation
self-reliance	the tendency to make do with one's own resources and not depend on help from others
sense of humor	an ability to see the potential for comedy in oneself and in most situations; the ability to appreciate the humor of others
serenity	the ability to remain calm and tranquil during potentially stressful moments
spirituality	the sense that there are more important things in life than physical existence
spontaneity	the capacity to behave comfortably in an extemporaneous manner
team-spirit	a willingness to work cooperatively with others and, when necessary, to put the good of the group ahead of one's personal good
thoughtfulness	a ready tendency to think of the needs, interests, and desires of others
thrift	frugality or a conservative approach to financial expenditures
trust	a tendency to believe others and to see the best in others
trustworthiness	acting in such a way as to earn the trust and confidence of others
uniqueness	being utterly unlike others, highly individualistic, and comfortable in one's own difference from the crowd

vision	the capacity to see possibilities that others may miss
vitality	a high level of energy and good health
wisdom	a level of understanding and insight into the world that goes beyond formal learning
wit	a wry and sophisticated sense of humor
wonder	a sense of awe and respect for the physical world, human capacity for achievement, or some other entity that is greater than the self
youthfulness	regardless of physical age, the tendency to demonstrate the level of energy and spirit commonly associated with the young

Table 2.2.   General Vices, Character Flaws, and Negative Traits

*Read over the list of vices, character flaws, and negative traits, and select five (and only five) that disturb, concern, offend, or annoy you more than others. Like table 2.1, the following list is not intended to be exhaustive. To the contrary, it has been pared down in such a way to avoid as much duplication and overlap as possible. For example, rather than treating **greed**, **avarice**, and **covetousness** as three separate qualities, they are intentionally conjoined in this list because, in common usage, they often refer to very similar behaviors. For this reason, if you don't find a value on this list that you expect to see, try looking for a synonym or close alternative.*

After you have narrowed down your list to only five items, identify the value or principle that you believe is most opposed to each vice you have selected.

aggression	engaging in inappropriately threatening behavior or actions
arrogance	excessive self-importance or conceit that results in contempt or disregard for others
bigotry	unwarranted bias or prejudice toward another group, particularly in such areas as politics, religion, and ethnicity, by someone who refuses to accept different views
boastfulness	referring immodestly to possessions or achievements; talking with excessive pride about an achievement or possession
callousness	showing no concern that other people are or might be hurt, upset, or made uncomfortable by one's actions
corruption	exploiting one's power or position for personal gain
cowardice	acting in a weak, excessively fearful, or spineless manner
cruelty	deliberately and remorselessly causing pain or anguish; acting in a manner that is needlessly harsh or severe
decadence	engaging in self-indulgence to a point that others regard as excessive, immoral, or harmful

deceitfulness	intentionally misleading or fraudulent
dishonesty	the use of lies, deceit, or cheating, particularly for personal gain
disloyalty	failing to honor one's commitments to a person, organization, or cause
disrespect	failure to give others the deference and degree of politeness they deserve
envy	excessive longing for someone else's success, good fortune, qualities, or possessions
gluttony	eating and drinking to excess; doing anything to the point of wastefulness
greed	an overwhelming desire to have more of something (often but not exclusively money) than is actually necessary
hypocrisy	acting in ways that are contrary to one's stated beliefs or values
immorality	behavior that violates accepted norms, often (although not exclusively) in the sphere of sexual activity
impatience	a tendency to be annoyed at being kept waiting or by being delayed
incompetence	lacking even the basic skills, resources, or abilities necessary to perform a task properly
infidelity	unfaithfulness or disloyalty, especially to a sexual or romantic partner
inflexibility	a stubborn unwillingness to change an opinion, point of view, or course of action
injustice	unfair or inequitable treatment of others
jealousy	excessive longing for someone else's romantic or sexual partner
laziness	an unwillingness to do necessary work or make a necessary effort
manipulation	the use of clever or devious means to control or influence someone
moodiness	the habit of being temperamental and changeable in terms of one's disposition
obsession	the state of becoming so preoccupied with a particular idea, person, or thing that this compulsion interferes with one's other activities
promiscuity	behavior characterized by casual and indiscriminate sexual activity, often with many people in succession
rage	the tendency to give in to an unreasonable amount of anger, often suddenly or with little provocation
resentfulness	the tendency to hold grudges

rudeness	the tendency to act in a disagreeable or discourteous manner
self-pity	wallowing in absorption with one's own problems and suffering, often in the belief that they are worse or more significant than those of others
selfishness	concern with one's own interests, needs, and wishes while ignoring those of others
thievery	absconding with someone else's possession
treason	betrayal of the allegiance owed to one's own country
unpredictability	behaving erratically or departing from one's usual pattern of behavior in an unpredictable manner
untrustworthiness	acting in a way that is not deserving of others' trust or confidence
wastefulness	the habit of consuming resources unwisely or lavishly
weakness	lack of strength, power, or determination

Table 2.3. Virtues, Values, or Principles Commonly Discussed in Higher Education

Read over the list of values, virtues, or core principles commonly mentioned in higher education, and select four that resonate with you more than others. Like the other two tables that precede it, the following list is not intended to be exhaustive. It merely represents a few of the most important ideals that motivate faculty members and administrators at colleges and universities.

academic freedom	"the freedom of university faculty to produce and disseminate knowledge through research, teaching, and service, without undue constraint" (Association of American Universities, 2013)
accountability	a sense of responsibility to one's discipline and institution for all of one's actions, often even extending to a sense of responsibility for what one's students, colleagues, and employees do
administrative accessibility	the belief that academic leaders should be as approachable and accessible as possible to faculty members (and perhaps students as well); the conviction that any faculty member (and possibly any student) can take whatever issue he or she wishes to the relevant administrator without having to go through unnecessary layers of bureaucracy
chain of command	respect for the authority of those above oneself in the institutional hierarchy; following proper procedures and reporting relationships; avoiding end runs; adherence to the policies and decisions of supervisors

citizen development	the idea that a primary—if not *the* primary—role of the college or university is to develop an educated and informed citizenry and that an institution or discipline that does not do so fails in one of its most important responsibilities
collegiality	"[O]pportunities for faculty members to feel that they belong to a mutually respected community of scholars who value each faculty member's contribution to the institution and feel concern for their colleagues' well-being" (Gappa, Austin, & Trice, 2007, 305)
community engagement	a commitment to the idea that colleges and universities should serve, not merely enrolled students, but the communities in which they are located and, by extension, the needs of humanity as a whole
confidentiality	preserving the privacy of information that is shared with one; keeping the secrets of others, particularly in a professional setting
culture of mentoring	dedication to the goal of serving the good of the academic community by providing a constructive and supportive environment where those who are more experienced mentor those who are less experienced, regardless of whether this relationship is between faculty members, students, or a faculty member and a student
data-informed culture	a commitment to basing all decisions on information that can be verified and replicated
discipline/field orientation	placing primary emphasis on the needs of one's area of specialty; the belief that one's academic field is of singular importance, even when compared to other academic areas
diversity	the conviction that higher education is enhanced by the widespread participation in it of people from different cultures, ethnicities, social classes, political convictions, and philosophical or religious beliefs
empiricism	the belief that all knowledge is ultimately derived from what can be perceived by the senses
evidence-based reasoning	a commitment to follow the evidence wherever it leads, even if that evidence challenges or disproves previously held beliefs and convictions
faculty-centeredness	the belief that an institution is, in essence, its faculty and that the core of an institution could survive without its students, administration, and physical plant but not without its faculty
faith-based learning	a belief that certain matters are ultimately unknowable or not understandable by human beings and simply must be accepted on faith

holistic orientation	the idea that a primary—if not *the* primary—role of the college or university is to develop "the whole person" and that a complete experience in higher education consists of a balance of curricular, co-curricular, and extracurricular activities
institutional autonomy	the conviction that institutions of higher learning should be free from external influence (for example, from political or religious entities) or, as defined by the United States Supreme Court in *Sweezy v. New Hampshire* (1957), "the right of the university to determine for itself, on academic grounds, who may teach, what may be taught, how it shall be taught, and who may be admitted to study" (cf. Association of American Universities, 2013)
instructional integrity	the principle that no one should claim to be an expert in an area in which he or she would not be recognized for expertise by appropriate trained and credentialed peers, that one should pursue the highest standards of honesty in one's teaching, that one should acknowledge the sources of one's information, and that one should make the greatest possible effort to ensure student success in learning
liberal arts orientation	a belief in the fundamental importance of the liberal arts and humanities in the intellectual development of every college-educated person
lifelong learning	the principle that one's education does not stop with one's formal schooling but continues throughout the person's life, often coupled with a belief that one of the most important benefits of a college education is a commitment to continuing education and a set of skills that makes it possible to pursue this goal
objectivity	impartiality and freedom from bias in the ways in which conclusions are drawn from available evidence
political correctness	the belief that care is warranted lest one's words or actions offend, even unintentionally, members of other nations, ethnicities, social or economic classes, levels of physical challenge, and religious beliefs
positive faculty-staff relationships	a commitment to constructive and respectful interactions between members of the faculty and staff with recognition that, although they may play different roles at an institution, each role is vitally important
positive faculty-student relationships	a commitment to constructive and respectful interactions between faculty members and students with recognition that, although they may play different roles at an institution, each role is vitally important
professional development	the conviction that members of the faculty, staff, and administration must continue to improve their professional skills throughout their entire careers by

	participating in conferences, workshops, and other formal training opportunities
pursuit of excellence	a commitment to the highest standards of quality with regard to all aspects of teaching and learning; the belief that, within reasonable limits, cost should not be an object when it comes to pursuing excellence in teaching and research
research integrity	a commitment to honesty in the performance of research and the dissemination of results, including the accurate acknowledgment of the roles played by other scholars in one's research
research orientation	a focus on research, scholarship, and creative activity as the single-most important component of academic life; dedication to the life of the mind, appreciation of intellectual pursuits, and esteem for the academic and creative contributions of others
school spirit	a sense of loyalty and devotion to a specific academic institution, often (although not exclusively) demonstrated by enthusiastic support of its athletic teams
shared governance	the belief that an institution's faculty, administration, and governing board all have clear roles in the governing of an institution and in its decision-making processes
student-centeredness	the belief that the education of students is the first and most significant role of higher education and that all decisions must ultimately be made by determining whether a given course of action is in the best interests of students
teaching-first orientation	the idea that, of the three roles of a college or university (teaching, research, and service), the teaching role takes precedence over the other two
transparency	a dedication to candor and openness in the way in which decisions are made
vocational orientation	the idea that a primary—if not *the* primary—role of the college or university is to make students employable and that an institution or discipline that does not do so fails in one of its most important responsibilities

Since some of these values may be identical to those you identified from table 2.1, you should end the thought experiment with a list of no fewer than nine but no more than fourteen principles that you regard as most important to you. If you complete the thought experiment with fewer than fourteen principles, you may at your option incorporate more than four items from table 2.3 until your total list includes up to fourteen items.

Merely identifying these core values is, of course, not enough. We must also test them to determine whether your decisions and actions actually reflect the principles that you believe are most important. And it is to that task that we shall turn in the next section of this book.

KEY POINTS FROM CHAPTER 2

- Our motivation for various actions can depend on our focus on the ultimate product we are trying to create or goal we are trying to achieve, the process we are using to create that product or achieve that goal, or the principles that cause us to act in a certain way.
- Robert House's Path-Goal Theory provides a useful framework for understanding product-oriented motivation.
- The problem with too exclusive a focus on product is that it can lead people to assume that the end justifies the means.
- Douglas McGregor's Theory X and Theory Y, combined with William Ouchi's Theory Z, provide a useful framework for understanding process-oriented motivation.
- A focus on either product or process is an "End-Pulling" Leadership Approach: In order to achieve some goal or improve some process, the leader is pulled along a particular path. A focus on principle, however, is a "Foundation-Pushing" Leadership Approach: The leader's attachment to certain ideals propels him or her in a certain direction.
- In order for an academic leadership approach to be authentic, it must follow from a leader's core values. Therefore, leaders must first understand what their core values are.
- Two initial ways of identifying your core values involve introspection. The first way is to answer questions or respond to statements in an online inventory, allowing the logarithm built into the inventory to calculate the results and rank your core principles. The other way is to scan through lists of virtues and vices, identifying the virtues that particularly resonate with you and the vices that particularly trouble you.

REFERENCES

Association of American Universities. (2013). Academic principles: A brief introduction. https://www.aau.edu/WorkArea/DownloadAsset.aspx?id=14364.

Berens, R. (n.d.). Forté Dreams Coaching: A really, really long list of possible values. http://www.fortedreams.com/a-really-really-long-list-of-possible-values.

Brown, D., & Crace, R. K. (1996). Life values inventory. http://www.uwgb.edu/outreach/socialwork/assets/pdf/Trauma2015/9_LifeValues.pdf.

Buller, J. L. (2015). *Change leadership in higher education: A practical guide to academic transformation.* San Francisco: Jossey-Bass.

Covey, S. R. (1989). *The seven habits of highly effective people: Restoring the character ethic.* New York: Simon and Schuster.

Gappa, J. M., Austin, A. E., & Trice, A. G. (2007). *Rethinking faculty work: Higher education's strategic imperative.* San Francisco: Jossey-Bass.

House, R. J. (1996). Path-goal theory of leadership: Lessons, legacy, and a reformulated theory. *Leadership Quarterly. 7*(3), 323–52.

House, R. J., & Mitchell, T. R. (1974). Path-goal theory of leadership. *Journal of Contemporary Business. 3*, 1–97.

McGregor, D. (1960). *The human side of enterprise.* New York: McGraw Hill.

Miller, W. R., C'de Baca, J., Matthews, D. B., & Wilbourne, P. L. (2001). Personal values card sort. http://www.motivationalinterviewing.org/sites/default/files/valuescardsort_0.pdf.

Ouchi, W. G. (1981). *Theory Z: How American business can meet the Japanese challenge.* Reading, MA: Addison-Wesley.

University of Pennsylvania: Authentic Happiness Questionnaire Center. (2017). https://www.authentichappiness.sas.upenn.edu/testcenter.

UQ Power. (2014). Personal values inventory. https://www.google.com/search?client=safari&rls=en&q=personal+values+inventory&ie=UTF-8&oe=UTF-8.

Writeworld. (n.d.). Huge list of vices. http://writeworld.tumblr.com/viceslist.

RESOURCES

Rifenbary, J. (2014). *No excuse!: Incorporating core values, accountability, and balance into your life and career.* (4th Ed.). Hummelstown, PA: Possibility Press.

Simon, S. B., Howe, L. W., & Kirschenbaum, H. (1995). *Values clarification.* New York: Warner Books.

Taylor, L. E. (2010). *The core values handbook: A primary manual for learning about the Core Values Index (CVI).* Tukwila, WA: Taylor Protocols.

Part II

The Crucible

THREE
The Core of Your Being

Core passions and aspirations should be consistent and in sync.

—Lorii Myers (2013) 32

We ended part I of this book by having you identify a list of nine or more principles that you regard as your core values. But there are times as an academic leader when even nine core values is too many to provide you with clear guidance about the best course of action to take. Authentic academic leaders know themselves well enough to realize that, in truly difficult situations, there's an even smaller subset of principles that reflect who they really are and what matters most to them.

In part II, we'll try to pare down your longer list of core values to identify what we'll call your **authentic values**: those two to four principles to which you return again and again when you're facing a challenging problem or feeling pressure to act in a way that you don't regard as appropriate for yourself.

There are two fundamental approaches that can be used to recognize your authentic values among your longer list of core values:

- *commitment*: reflecting on your core values and categorizing them according to the level of commitment you believe you have to each of them;
- *conflict*: imagining situations where two or more of your core values are placed in conflict with one another and then determining which value you'd give priority to over the other(s).

In this chapter, we'll explore the approach of commitment, deferring our examination of conflict until the next chapter.

THE KRATHWOHL AFFECTIVE DOMAIN TAXONOMY

Most people reading this book are probably quite familiar with *Bloom's Taxonomy*, the hierarchy of learning and understanding developed by the educational psychologist Benjamin Bloom (1913–1999) that builds from lower-level thinking skills (knowledge, comprehension, and application) to higher order thinking skills (analysis, synthesis, and evaluation) (Bloom, 1956). They may even be aware of revisions to and expansions of this taxonomy made by Lorin Anderson, David Krathwohl, L. Dee Fink, and others (Anderson, Krathwohl, et al. 2000 and 2001; Fink 2003).

But what they may not be aware of is that Bloom did not envision the taxonomy so commonly associated with his name to be the *only* taxonomy that educators could use to help their students develop and mature. What is referred to today as Bloom's Taxonomy is actually *Bloom's Cognitive Taxonomy*, and the author identified two other domains—the *psychomotor domain* (physical skills and coordination) and the *affective domain* (emotions and attitudes)—that could also be used in setting educational objectives.

It's the last of these domains that concerns us here because it's in the affective domain that Bloom and others posited that people develop an understanding of and appreciation for *values*.

In 1973, the educational psychologist David Krathwohl, along with Bertram Masia and Bloom himself, published an extension to the famous cognitive domain taxonomy that took a similar approach with the affective domain. Now known as the **Krathwohl Affective Domain Taxonomy** (or, more simply, **Krathwohl's Taxonomy**), this approach creates a hierarchy of emotional commitment to emotions and values that ranges from mere awareness of these concepts to full embodiment of them in one's life and identity. (See figure 3.1.)

Like the cognitive domain taxonomy, this affective domain taxonomy has also undergone some revision as scholars have recognized important components that the original version was missing. For example, Steve Lang and Judy Wilkerson (2008) added an additional level at the bottom of Krathwohl's Taxonomy. Calling this level "Unaware," Lang and Wilkerson wanted to indicate that there are some values that certain people

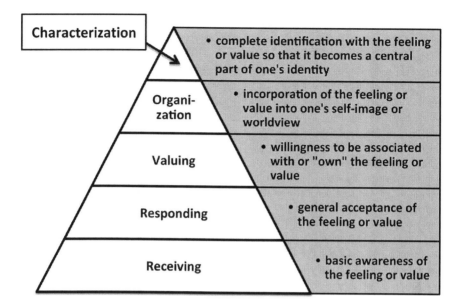

Figure 3.1. The Krathwohl Affective Domain Taxonomy: Original Version

either don't know or care about even enough to rise to Krathwohl's level of "Receiving."

I was once conducting a workshop on work-life balance at which a university president, who was a well-known workaholic, asked (in genuine confusion and with absolutely no sarcasm), "I just don't understand what we've been talking about today. What do you mean when you say 'work-life balance'? I've never heard of it." There were a lot of eyes rolling among the other participants at that point and an exchange of looks that seemed to imply, "Well, *that* explains a thing or two."

In addition, we might add an extra level at the top of the taxonomy, one that we'll call "Obsessing," to indicate an unhealthy preoccupation or obsession with a specific feeling or value. The Roman Catholic Church often speaks of *scrupulosity*: the tendency to become overly critical of oneself or obsessive about confessing one's perceived sins. People who are scrupulous in this sense take the value of wanting to become as free from sin as possible to a destructive or injurious degree.

Because of these enhancements to Krathwohl's original taxonomy, we'll use a modified form of it in this chapter that appears in table 3.1. As you see in the table, our approach also omits Krathwohl's concern for both feelings and values, focusing only on values or principles.

APPLYING THE REVISED AFFECTIVE DOMAIN TAXONOMY

In order to use this revised taxonomy to help isolate your authentic values from your other core values, it would be best if the exercise dealt specifically with the nine or more values you identified in chapter 2. But, of course, I have no way of knowing what they are. And it's not practical to invent an exercise that covers all 150 possible values that can be found in tables 2.1, 2.2, and 2.3. This book would need to be massive to accommodate such an exercise, and it probably wouldn't be worth your time to engage in it.

So, we're going to conduct a far more focused experiment that addresses twelve of the general principles and higher educational values that are mentioned in chapter 2. These selections should be sufficient to give you a good idea about how the revised Krathwohl taxonomy works and can be applied to evaluating your level of commitment to each core value you identified.

For the following exercise, read the description of the value or principle that is introduced and then choose *one and only one* of the sentences following it that *most closely* reflects your own attitude toward that value or principle. It's quite possible that none of the statements will be an

Table 3.1.   The Krathwohl Affective Domain Taxonomy: Revised Version

Designation	Description
Obsessing or Scrupulous	The person is overly fixated on this value/principle and is preoccupied with it to an unhealthy degree.
Characterizing	The person is fully committed to this value/principle.
Organizing	The person is taking active steps to embody this value/principle in his or her actions and life.
Valuing	The person is sufficiently committed to this value/principle that he or she is willing to be associated with it.
Responding	The person has a relatively low level of commitment to this value/principle.
Receiving	The person is generally aware of the significance of this value/principle.
Pre-receiving or Unaware	The person either doesn't know or doesn't care about this value/principle.

exact reflection of your own level of commitment. Simply choose which-ever statement is the most similar to how you yourself feel.

1. **Integrity**, for the purposes of this exercise, will be defined as the quality of being honest, transparent, fair to all, and consistent in adhering to a deeply held set of moral values.

   a. I think that integrity is an important trait for an academic leader to have, and I demonstrate it when others call it to my attention.
   b. Integrity is an important quality for academic leaders but I find that the pressures of the job often mean that I can pay it relatively little attention.
   c. It's fine to give lip service to vague concepts like integrity but academic leadership is really about getting the job done, regardless of what it takes.
   d. Integrity is the principle that guides everything I do and every decision I make as an academic leader. It defines who I am, and I hope it will be seen as a major part of my legacy.
   e. I am so disturbed when other academic leaders act without integrity that I bring these actions to their attention without concern for the effect it may have on my career or the welfare of my program.
   f. I try to demonstrate integrity in everything I do as an academic leader and am proud when someone says that I've acted with integrity.
   g. I try to act as a role model of integrity in everything I do as an academic leader and to assist others with their own efforts to act with integrity.

2. **Work-Life Balance**, for the purposes of this exercise, will be defined as the concept of giving proper attention to both *work* (career and public life) and personal *life* (health, leisure, family, friends, and spiritual or philosophical values).

   a. I'm always attracted to the idea of work-life balance, but I'm just not very good at it.
   b. I not only value work-life balance for myself, but I also encourage it in my friends and colleagues.

   c. I plan my schedule carefully so that I always have enough time not only to meet my work commitments but also to relax, take care of my health, and give family or friends the attention they deserve.

   d. If I find myself devoting even a little bit too much time to work or to my personal needs, I feel that my whole day is ruined—maybe even my week or month.

   e. I'm doing better at work-life balance than I once did. Now at least when people call my attention to my lapses in this regard, I take steps to do better.

   f. Other people often tell me that they're surprised by how much I get done at work, never missing deadlines but also having plenty of time to do the things that enrich my personal life.

   g. People who talk about work-life balance are talking about an illusion. You either care about your job or you care about your personal interests. You can't accommodate both.

3. **Pursuit of Excellence**, for the purposes of this exercise, will be defined as the drive not just to become better but to become the best or preeminent either overall or in a specific area of endeavor.

   a. I often promise myself that I'll work harder and be more creative so that our program will become better, but other priorities always seem to get in the way.

   b. I rarely let a week go by when I don't make some specific effort that I believe will cause our program to become recognized as the best.

   c. Even though many of my colleagues seem to regard just getting by as being good enough, I feel that I have higher standards. I'm often the person who says we can do better.

   d. We simply *have* to be the best at what we do. If we slipped in the rankings even a little or if I thought other programs were passing us by, I don't know if I could handle it.

e. People associated with other programs similar to ours often ask me what we did so as to improve so quickly and become preeminent.

f. No matter how hard you work, someone is always going to be better than you. So, don't worry about it. Let other people win the rat race. It's not worth it to me.

g. Our strategic plan and other institutional initiatives lay out a clear pathway to excellence, and I'm in full compliance with any requirement they have for my area.

4. **Academic Freedom**, for the purposes of this exercise, will be defined as personal not institutional academic freedom or, namely, the belief that scholars should be free to teach and communicate ideas, facts, and perspectives without interference from university administrators, political forces, or any agency other than their own expertise and professional judgment.

a. I simply can't tolerate anyone even having the impression that academic freedom isn't the single most important right we have in higher education. If someone in my life speaks slightingly of academic freedom, our relationship is over.

b. It is not an exaggeration to say that my desire to preserve academic freedom affects everything I do in higher education and every choice I make as an academic leader.

c. Academic freedom is significant enough that, if asked to serve on a committee charged with protecting it, I'd probably agree to serve.

d. I try to get elected or appointed to faculty or administrative bodies that seek to defend academic freedom, and I review the news and pronouncements of our administration to determine if academic freedom is being seriously threatened.

e. Academic freedom is really a myth. Higher education would survive just fine without it. If you show up for work and do your job, you'll be fine.

f. More than once, I've had to be the person who had to speak in defense of academic freedom at a public meeting.

g. Intellectually, I accept that academic freedom is important, but the fact is that I rarely think of it, and it doesn't affect my life very much.

5. **Accessibility**, for the purposes of this exercise, will be defined as the degree of availability and approachability an academic leader has to his or her stakeholders.

a. People always talk about their "open door policies," but you can't be accessible to everyone and still get your job done as an academic leader.

b. Whenever someone says they needed me but I wasn't available, it bothers me so much that I often can't sleep until I've been able to meet with that person, apologize, and make it right.

c. Having other people know that I'm easily approachable and that they can talk to me about anything is a goal, but I'm often so busy that I need to shut my door or work some place where I won't be disturbed.

d. Accessibility is the principle that guides everything I do and every decision I make as an academic leader. It defines who I am to the extent that I'd like to be known as Dr. Accessible.

e. I take active steps to be as accessible to others as I can such as blocking out time every day to be readily available, notifying people about how best to reach me, and trying to avoid activities that might make me inaccessible for too long a time.

f. I appreciate it when other academic leaders are accessible, and I try to emulate them whenever I can.

g. I tell faculty members in my area that they should feel free to talk to me anytime they have issues or problems.

6. **Compassion**, for the purposes of this exercise, will be defined as the ability to share, understand, and appreciate the feelings of others; caring for others; and concern for their well-being.

a. I'm commonly considered to be the single most compassionate person in our program—perhaps at our entire school.

b. I'm often the one who provides the "voice of compassion" at meetings.

c. I still regularly lose sleep over times when I wasn't as compassionate as I should have been, even though some of those incidents occurred ten or twenty years ago.

d. Compassion is really out of place when it comes to higher education. Our job is to hold others to high standards not to make allowances for them when they fail to achieve important goals.

e. I believe in compassion and am distressed when others point out that I've failed to be compassionate in a given situation.

f. Whenever I interact with a student or colleague, I ask myself, "Am I being as compassionate as I should be?"

g. I really wish I could say I were more compassionate, but the stresses of life today make compassion more of an ideal than a personal achievement for me.

7. **Gratitude**, for the purposes of this exercise, will be defined as a willingness to express appreciation for the efforts of others and a tendency to act upon that willingness.

a. We go around thanking people all too much in higher education. Doing your job shouldn't earn you thanks and praise. It already earns you your paycheck, your grade in the course, or the right to keep your job.

b. More than once, someone has pointed out that I haven't been appreciative enough of his or her efforts, and I took steps to correct that oversight as soon as I could.

c. I probably thank others more than do many of my colleagues.

d. I believe that gratitude is important, and I would like to show it more, but I often forget to do so.

e. Thanking people and demonstrating gratitude is an important part of the way I work. You might call gratitude one of my "standard operating procedures."

f. I can recall times when I got home, realized I forgot to thank someone, and drove across town to express gratitude even though I had many other things to do and the person I thanked didn't consider it that important.

g. It's not uncommon for people to thank me for taking the time to thank them. In fact, that's an experience I have several times a week.

8. **Professionalism**, for the purposes of this exercise, will be defined as acting in a manner that is expected in the business world or other professional settings.

a. Professionalism drives the way I work, think, and interact with others. To the best of my knowledge, no one would ever consider me as unprofessional in any way.

b. A college or university is simply not a professional environment like a corporate office or court of law. It's a creative, messy, constantly evolving environment that is distorted once we start expecting people to dress, talk, and act according to artificial "professional" standards.

c. Although I've been called unprofessional at times, I'm actively working to improve my behavior in this area.

d. On several occasions I've found fault with colleagues for being unprofessional.

e. I admire professionalism. I just wish I could say that I demonstrated it more.

f. Others have cited me as a model of professionalism, and that type of praise makes me very happy.

g. If someone said that anything I did was unprofessional—even once—I would find it so unbearable that I couldn't look that person in the face ever again. I might even have to leave my job or break off the relationship I had with that person.

9. **Diversity**, for the purposes of this exercise, will be defined as the conviction that higher education is enhanced by the widespread participation in it of people from different cultures, ethnicities, social classes, political convictions, and philosophical or religious beliefs.

    a. I would put my job, the success of our program, and even the survival of our institution in jeopardy if I felt it necessary to do so as a way of promoting greater diversity in higher education.

    b. Even though some people may feel that I place too great an importance on achieving diversity among the faculty and students, I take their criticism as a compliment.

    c. I regularly use my desire to improve the diversity of our faculty and student body as a guiding principle. To me, the diversity someone can bring our environment often outranks his or her past achievements and other factors.

    d. Diversity has become a fetish in higher education. By their very nature, colleges and universities are not diverse communities: They exclude those who do not have the intellectual capacity to succeed there. Trying to accommodate other types of diversity just distracts us from our true mission: the creation and transmission of knowledge.

    e. When others speak about the need for diversity among the faculty or student body, I often concur.

    f. On search committees or when discussing the admission of students, I'm often the one who tries to make a case for greater diversity.

    g. I believe that a diverse faculty and student body is important. But when you're also trying to recruit the right students and the best faculty members, diversity often gets placed on a back burner.

10. **Objectivity**, for the purposes of this exercise, will be defined as impartiality and freedom from bias in the ways in which conclusions are drawn from available evidence.

a. When I read articles about members of the faculty or administration at some school who have failed to be as objective as they should be, it disturbs me.

b. Any implication that I've failed to be completely objective at all times would cause me to question my choice of careers, even my sense of self-worth.

c. Many people have told me that, when they need a perfectly objective point of view, they come to me.

d. I strive to be objective whenever I can, but I know that I often don't succeed.

e. There *is* no such thing as objectivity in any human endeavor. Even in the most data-driven environments, the perspective of the observer or interpreter will always distort the evidence.

f. I'm surprised by how often my colleagues don't see themselves as failing to be objective even though I easily recognize how subjectivity has distorted their observations.

g. In both my professional work and my personal life, I evaluate each decision on the basis of whether I was sufficiently objective in reaching a conclusion.

11. **Patriotism**, for the purposes of this exercise, will be defined as love of one's country, its achievements, and its values.

a. Patriotism is, in my opinion, the greatest obligation a citizen has. It should guide our actions, our beliefs, and our policies at all times.

b. On major national holidays, I must admit that I do feel a bit patriotic.

c. It wouldn't surprise me if, when other people thought about those on our campus who are particularly patriotic, they think of me.

d. Patriotism is just what people call their nationalism or chauvinism. It frequently degenerates into xenophobia and leads to fear or hatred of others. I'd rather be considered an internationalist or a "citizen of the world."

e. It bothers me when I see how little patriotic sentiment moves many of my colleagues and those of my community.

f. Being patriotic always sounds like a good thing, but I think of myself more in terms of my profession, family, or local community than in terms of national values.

g. I can't understand why people wouldn't love their country, salute its flag, or serve it in any way they can. If it were up to me, unpatriotic actions would be crimes, punishable by prison, expulsion—or worse.

12. **Faith**, for the purposes of this exercise, will be defined as commitment to beliefs that cannot be proven by experience or reasoning.

a. I can think of a number of times in my life when faith provided me with comfort, strength, or the guidance I needed.

b. My single greatest mission in life is to convert others to my faith. Because it is important to me, it can be important for everyone else, too. In fact, I don't believe that you can be a good person without faith. I'd certainly never vote for, work with, or respect someone who said he or she had doubts about the importance of faith.

c. Faith is merely a polite term for gullibility. Having faith is inimical to our goals as academic professionals. We have to be committed to the truth wherever the data and logic lead us. Once you decide to accept something on faith, you accept it as true without evidence, and doing so violates our whole purpose as academics.

d. I'm widely regarded as a spiritual person for whom faith is an important aspect of life.

e. I wish I had a greater sense of faith. It seems to help other people, but I just find it difficult to believe in something without much evidence.

f. When I'm experiencing trouble or when I'm talking to someone who is very spiritual, I feel my own faith rekindling.

g. I can honestly say that faith is the most important part of my life. It defines who I am, how I respond to others, and how I see the world.

INTERPRETING YOUR RESULTS

Table 3.2 indicates how you should interpret your results for the inventory you just completed. The numbers of the columns at the top indicate the question; the letter of your answer is paired with one of the categories on the revised Krathwohl Affective Domain Taxonomy.

Values that, for you, reached the levels of "Valuing," "Organizing," or "Characterizing" (though not "Obsessing" or "Scrupulous") may be good candidates for your highly selective set of authentic values. Values that you responded only on the levels of "Responding," "Receiving," or "Pre-Receiving"/"Unaware" almost certainly don't belong among your authentic values, and probably not even among your larger set of core values.

It's difficult to establish a hard and fast rule because each person completes the inventory with slightly different assumptions about how rigorously to evaluate each choice that's presented, but a general guideline might be that authentic values should be ones that rise to the level of

Table 3.2.   Interpreting the Exercise on the Modified Krathwohl Taxonomy

	1	*2*	*3*	*4*	*5*	*6*	*7*	*8*	*9*	*10*	*11*	*12*
Obsessing or Scrupulous	e	d	d	a	b	c	f	g	a	b	g	b
Characterizing	f	f	e	b	d	a	g	f	e	c	a	g
Organizing	d	c	b	d	e	f	e	a	c	g	c	d
Valuing	g	b	c	f	g	b	c	d	f	f	e	a
Responding	a	e	g	c	f	e	b	c	e	a	b	f
Receiving	b	a	a	g	c	g	d	e	g	d	f	e
Pre-receiving or Unaware	c	g	f	e	a	d	a	b	d	e	d	c

"Organizing" or "Characterizing," while core values should at least reach the level of "Valuing."

Because so many values were listed in tables 2.1, 2.2, and 2.3, it's possible that none of the principles addressed in the inventory you just completed appear on your list of core values. But the revised Krathwohl Affective Domain Taxonomy can still be used to assess your level of commitment to those values. Simply ask yourself the following questions about each value on your list:

a. Do you find yourself fixating on your need to embody this principle, unable to relax or forgive yourself if you don't live up to your expectations? If so, then the value probably rises to the level of "Obsessing"/"Scrupulous" for you. Such a principle may not be a good choice for one of your authentic values because you may have such an unhealthy preoccupation with it that it affects your decisions even when other considerations may be more important.

b. Does the principle embody who you are as a person, revealing itself to be an important part of your identity? Would you really not be recognizable as yourself if you violated this principle? If so, then the value probably rises to the level of "Characterizing" for you. As such, it may well be one of your authentic values.

c. Does the principle guide your decisions on a regular basis? If so, then the value probably rises to the level of "Organizing" for you. As such, it could be one of your authentic values and almost certainly is one of your core values.

d. Do people often associate this principle with you? Are you often recognized for acting in accordance with it? If so, then the value probably rises to the level of "Valuing" for you. As such, it could be one of your core values.

e. Do you admire this principle and live up to it when your attention is called to it? If so, then the value probably rises to the level of "Responding" for you. As such, your commitment to it is probably too weak for it to be one of your core values.

f. Do you give lip service to the importance of this value, even if you don't think about it much when making decisions? If so, then the value probably rises to the level of "Receiving" for you. As such, your commitment to it is far too weak for it to be one of your core values.

g. Did you have to think about what this principle really means? Or do you regard the attention it receives from others as foolish or misguided in some way? If so, then the value is probably on the level of "Pre-Receiving"/"Unaware" for you. As such, your commitment to it is far too weak for it to be one of your values at all.

For any of the principles you included on your list of potential core values, see if you can honestly view them in the way described under b or c above. If not, go back to tables 2.1, 2.2, and 2.3 and try to identify other values that seem to characterize you better or around which you organize your life.

THE JOHARI WINDOW

Another useful tool for exploring your level of commitment to various values is the **Johari Window**. This technique wasn't originally developed to help individuals better understand their most important values; it was designed to improve teamwork.

In 1955, the psychologists Joseph Luft (1916–2014) and Harrington Ingham (1916–1995) created the Johari Window as a way for people to promote greater self-understanding and transparency as part of an organization, work group, or any other type of closely knit team. They called the tool they created the Johari Window by combining the casual form of their two first names: Joe and Harry.

But even though the device was originally designed for one purpose, it's actually quite effective in helping people identify their authentic values. We just have to use it in a modified form as we did with the Krathwohl Affective Domain Taxonomy.

To use the Johari Window, we should imagine a window with four panes. (See figure 3.2.) As we move from left to right in the window, we move from what we know about ourselves to what we hide about ourselves. As we move from top to bottom, we move from what others see in us to what we hide from others. In this way, the four panes of the window can be labeled as follows:

- the upper left pane: the **Open Self**, what you know about yourself and reveal to others;
- the upper right pane: the **Blind Self**, what you don't know about yourself, but others do;

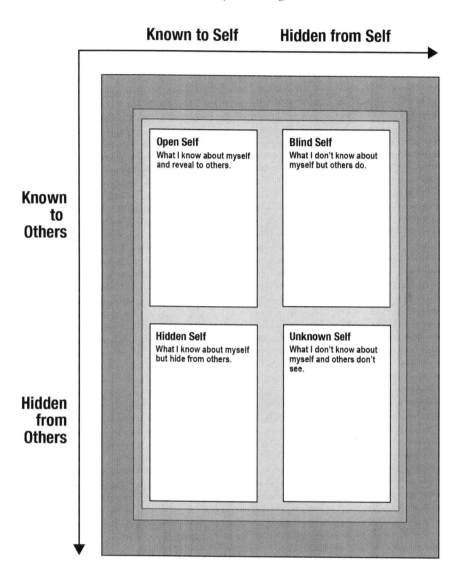

Figure 3.2.   The Johari Window

- the lower left pane: the **Hidden Self**, what you know about yourself, but hide from others;
- the lower right pane: the **Unknown Self**, what you don't know about yourself and others don't see.

In the original version of the Johari Window, each team member fills in the panes by selecting words from a list of fifty-six adjectives that he or she believes will best fall into those four different categories. Other members of the team then complete a Johari Window for each other member of the team.

When these windows are compared, each person gains insight into those qualities that he or she believes to be hidden or unrecognized, but that are actually known to everyone else in the group. As discussion of the Johari Window continues, the participants gain greater self-awareness, increase their levels of trust and transparency with others, and feel more comfortable revealing aspects of themselves that they formerly felt they needed to conceal.

Our modified exercise with the Johari Window will involve two variations. First, we'll use a much larger set of adjectives that appears in table 3.3. Second, we'll conduct the exercise without use of a team.

In the Johari Window that appears in figure 3.2, choose as many adjectives from table 3.3 that you believe are appropriate for each pane of the window. But here's the important restriction: You can only use each adjective *once*. You're free to omit as many adjectives from table 3.3 as you like. After all, there will probably be many qualities there that don't apply to you, at least not in any significant way.

But if you do use an adjective, you have to assign it to one and only one window. You have to declare whether you believe you demonstrate this quality openly and perceptibly to others, and you have to declare whether the quality is one that you willingly recognize in yourself or try to conceal from yourself. You're not permitted any equivocation, such as, "Well, I kind of demonstrate this quality publicly, and I kind of conceal it." If the quality applies to you, you have to take a specific stand by assigning it to only one of the windows.

You might make an objection to the ground rules for this exercise by asking, "If I hide a quality from myself, how can I possibly be aware of it? Aren't you asking me to do something that I can't possibly do?" The fact of the matter is that we're more aware of the qualities we "hide" from ourselves than we like to admit. For example, we may not like to admit to ourselves that we're selfish or moody, and we may not frequently dwell on how we embody these qualities, but in our most honest and self-reflective moments, we can become conscious of them.

If that strategy isn't enough to help you identify the qualities you think you're hiding from yourself, there's an old training technique that may help. Frequently in workshops when a participant is struggling with

Table 3.3.   Adjectives to Be Used with the Modified Johari Window

adaptable	envious	persistent
aggressive	ethical	politically correct
altruistic	experienced	practical
ambitious	faculty-oriented	professional
appreciative	fair	promiscuous
arrogant	faith-oriented	punctual
assertive	faithful	rational
bigoted	family-oriented	resentful
boastful	fit	reverent
brave/bold	frugal	rude
brilliant	generous	scholarly
callous	gluttonous	school-spirited
candid	greedy	self-controlled
charismatic	gregarious	self-pitying
clever	healthy	self-reliant
compassionate	hedonistic	selfish
composed	holistic	serene
confident	honest	sophisticated
confiding	honorable	spiritual
cooperative	hot-tempered	spontaneous
corrupt	humble	steadfast
courteous	humorous	stubborn
cowardly	hypocritical	student-oriented
creative	immoral	teaching-oriented
credulous	impatient	team-spirited
cruel	incompetent	thoughtful
data-oriented/data-driven	influential	tidy
deceitful	intelligent	traitorous
decisive	jealous	transparent
dependable	lazy	trusting
dignified	loyal	trustworthy
diligent	manipulative	unfair
dishonest	meticulous	unfaithful
disloyal	mindful	unique
disrespectful	moody	unpredictable

diversity-minded	neat	untrustworthy
earnest	noble-minded	visionary
educated	nonbureaucratic	vocationally oriented
effectual/effective	objective	wasteful
efficient	obsessive	weak
elegant	open-minded	wise
eloquent	optimistic	witty
empirical	passionate	young-at-heart
enthusiastic		

a particularly difficult question and repeatedly answering "I don't know," the trainer will try to shock an answer out of the person by asking, "Well, what would the answer be if you did know?" or (more kindly) "What do you imagine the answer might be if you did know?"

It's surprising the number of times participants will immediately answer the question when it's phrased in one of these forms even though only moments earlier they claimed they couldn't possibly know what to reply. They actually *did* know; it's just that they didn't want to commit themselves or some unconscious factor was holding them back.

It's much the same when it comes to completing your Johari Window. If you can't figure out how to complete the panes on the right side, ask yourself what you *imagine* to be in there. If a magician could somehow reveal to you the qualities others see in you but you don't see yourself, which qualities would least surprise you? And if the same magician could then expose the qualities that you think are so hidden in you that neither you nor anyone else can see them, which qualities might make you say, "Okay. I guess I can see that"?

With these instructions in mind, therefore, fill in your own personal Johari Window. Be sure to complete this exercise before moving on to the next section because, if you know in advance how we're going to use it, your answers may not be as candid as they would be without this knowledge. And, since our goal is to help you identify your most authentic self, it's important that your answers to this exercise be as candid and unguarded as possible.

USING THE MODIFIED JOHARI WINDOW

Once you've completed your Johari Window by drawing from the list of adjectives that appears in table 3.3, it's time to examine it and see what it reveals. The first thing to notice is why we used a different set of adjectives from those traditionally used with this exercise. The words you were instructed to use were based on the lists of general values and vices that appear in tables 2.1 and 2.2 and, to a lesser extent, the list of higher education concepts that appear in table 2.3.

In other words, the modified Johari Window causes us to take a second look at the values we explored earlier and to ask which of them we tend to demonstrate openly, which of them we tend to have but conceal, and which of them we don't even like to admit to ourselves that we have. In this way, you can look at your Johari Window and ask yourself the following questions:

- Which pane represents the closest approximation to my highly selective list of authentic values?
- Which list represents the closest approximation to my larger list of core values?
- If I were forced to choose one pane that best describes my "true self," which pane would that be?

The goal should be for the answer to all of these questions to be on the upper-half of your Johari Window, preferably in the "Open Self" pane on the upper left. That result would mean that the principles you identified as your core values and authentic values are actually guiding your actions. You're committed to them to a significant enough degree that others associate those qualities with you. It may be that, in certain cases, you'd like to believe you're not openly demonstrating those qualities even though, in your heart of hearts, you know you are.

In any case, if your core and authentic values are widely reflected in the top half of your Johari Window, your level of commitment to those principles seems high. Even better, if you believe that one of these panes is the best depiction of your "true self," you seem to be well on your way toward authentic academic leadership. The only question you might have is, if your "true self" is at the upper right rather than the upper left, what's preventing you from acknowledging these qualities to yourself more openly?

It's more problematic if your answer to any one of the three questions above involved the bottom half of the Johari Window. That would mean that the principles that, at the moment at least, you think are your core values or authentic values involve qualities that you conceal from others, perhaps even from yourself.

If that is the case, you have to wonder what your level of commitment is to these principles that you claim to be important to you. They don't appear to be guiding your actions to the extent that most people recognize those qualities in you. And if you don't even like to admit that you have those qualities, your commitment to them must be very weak indeed.

It may not be the end of the world if your "true self" is hidden from others; sometimes these parts of ourselves are so precious to us that we're reluctant to share them. But it does call into question how authentic you may be in your interactions with others if you're actively concealing important aspects central to your character. And it should be a red flag if your "true self" is something that you believe neither you nor anyone else can see. It should cause you to wonder why you can't bear to admit to anyone who you really are and why you yourself don't want to admit it.

If you assigned your "true self" to the lower-right pane of your Johari Window, you almost certainly have a lot more work to do in terms of understanding yourself and your motivations before you can even begin to practice authentic academic leadership.

DRAWING CONCLUSIONS

The approach that we've taken in this chapter, reflecting on our level of commitment to various values, is an important first step toward uncovering those values by which we ought to be leading authentically. After all, engaging in self-reflection is the first and most important of the central principles of values-based leadership that Harry Kraemer discusses in *From Values to Action* (Kraemer, 2011, 13–26). But reflection alone isn't enough. We don't always know ourselves and our motivations as well as we'd like.

There's a reason why one of the panes of the Johari Window is called the "Unknown Self," and there are parts of our nature that even the keenest introspection can't perceive. The best way to find those hidden dimensions of our beliefs is to put ourselves (metaphorically) into the crucible, test our convictions, and see what emerges from the process. And that's the task we'll turn to in the next chapter.

KEY POINTS FROM CHAPTER 3

- Within our set of core values, there's an even smaller subset of values that are particularly important to us: We call these two to four principles our *authentic values*.
- There are two approaches we can use to determine which of our core values tend to be most important to us: *commitment* (reflecting on our degree of dedication to each value in turn) and *conflict* (putting two or more values into conflict with one another and seeing which value we regularly choose).
- A modified form of the Krathwohl Affective Domain Taxonomy, originally developed by David Krathwohl, is a useful device for gauging the commitment level we have to various values.
- In the Modified Krathwohl Affective Domain Taxonomy, our authentic values rise to the level of "Characterizing" or, perhaps, "Organizing."
- Another technique we can use to determine our authentic values is a modified form of the Johari Window, originally developed by Joseph Luft and Harrington Ingham.
- On the modified Johari Window, the qualities we associate with our authentic values should appear on the upper half, most desirably in the upper-left pane, the area assigned to our "Open Self."

REFERENCES

Anderson, L. W., Krathwohl, D. R., Airasian, P. W., Cruikshank, K. A., Mayer, R. E., Pintrich, P. R., Raths, J., & Wittrock, M. C. (2000). *A taxonomy for learning, teaching, and assessing: A revision of Bloom's taxonomy of educational objectives*. Needham Heights, MA: Allyn & Bacon.

Anderson, L. W., Krathwohl, D. R., Airasian, P. W., Cruikshank, K. A., Mayer, R. E., Pintrich, P. R., Raths, J., & Wittrock, M C. (2001). *A taxonomy for learning, teaching, and assessing: A revision of Bloom's taxonomy of educational objectives*. Abridged edition. Needham Heights, MA: Allyn & Bacon.

Bloom, B. S. (1956). *Taxonomy of educational objectives. Handbook I: The cognitive domain*. New York: David McKay.

Fink, D. L. (2003). *Creating significant learning experiences*. San Francisco: Jossey-Bass.

Kraemer, H. M. J. (2011). *From values to action: The four principles of values-based leadership*. San Francisco: Jossey-Bass.

Krathwohl, D. R., Bloom, B. S., & Masia, B. B. (1973). *Taxonomy of educational objectives, the classification of educational goals, handbook II: Affective domain*. New York: David McKay.

Lang, W. S., & Wilkerson, J. R. (March 2008). Measuring teacher dispositions with different item structures: An application of the Rasch model to a complex accreditation requirement. Paper presented at the American Educational Research Association. New York: 1–50. http://files.eric.ed.gov/fulltext/ED502965.pdf.

Myers, L. (2013). *3 off the tee: No excuses: The fit mind-fit body strategy book*. Barrie, ON: Leda.

RESOURCES

George, B., Snook, S. A., & Craig, N. (2015). *The discover your true north fieldbook: A personal guide to finding your authentic leadership*. Hoboken, NJ: Wiley.

Krogerus, M., Tschäppeler, R., & Piening, J. (2012). *The decision book: Fifty models for strategic thinking*. New York: Norton.

Martin, K., & Osterling, M. (2014). *Value stream mapping: How to visualize work and align leadership for organizational transformation*. New York: McGraw-Hill.

FOUR

Dilemmas, Quandaries, and Predicaments

A moral dilemma is equally absorbing whether the stakes are the destiny of nations or the happiness of one or two people—at the most.
—Alexander McCall Smith, *A Conspiracy of Friends* (2013)

Repeatedly in their discussions of authentic leadership, authors like Bill George (2003), Sandy Shugart (2013), and Robert Thomas (2008) return to the notion of a *crucible* as the test of a person's values. Here, for example, is how George describes the importance of this concept:

> In his recent book *Geeks and Geezers,* author Warren Bennis observes that most of his interviewees passed through a crucible that tested them to the depths of their being and enabled the successes they realized later in life. Having survived, you will know that indeed you can take on any challenge and come out of it as a better person for the experience. (George, 2003, 27; citing Bennis and Thomas, 2002, 4–18)

In its most literal sense, a crucible is a container in which the contents are subjected to extremely high temperatures, often to refine them or to separate pure metals from the dross. Metaphorically, people undergo a crucible experience when they face a severe trial or test that proves their true worth or commitment to their core values. That, for instance, is the sense of the term that caused the playwright Arthur Miller (1915–2005) to call his 1953 play about the Salem witch trials, *The Crucible*.

Yet even beyond this general metaphor, there's another meaning of the term that attracts George, Shugart, Thomas, and others to the word *crucible*. A crucible was the container in which alchemists tried to turn base metals into gold by heating them in contact with the philosopher's stone (sometimes also called the *elixir*), a legendary substance that was believed to have special powers.

In this extended metaphor,

- the crucible represents a severe moral crisis,
- precious metals like gold represent a person's positive or more admirable characteristics,
- base metals like lead represent a person's vices or less admirable qualities, and
- the philosopher's stone or elixir represents the person's moral compass. (See, for example, Thomas, 2008, vii–viii; Shugart, 2013, 15.)

So, the idea is that, when we face a moral crisis, it's our moral compass—or, as we might now say, our authentic values—that helps bring our more positive qualities to the surface and that suppresses our negative impulses or less attractive qualities.

The best way, therefore, for me to test the next level of your commitment to the values you've identified as central to you is to subject you to a moral crisis. But that wouldn't be ethical on my part (and it certainly wouldn't pass the criteria of my university's Institutional Review Board), so we'll have to try to accomplish this goal by another means. And fortunately there's a widely accepted alternative method available to us, an exercise known as **Kohlberg Dilemmas.**

KOHLBERG DILEMMAS

Lawrence Kohlberg (1927–1987) was an American psychologist who developed a theory of moral development that posited that children and young adults develop a sense of right and wrong in six stages.

1. **Obedience and the Fear of Punishment**. The child's critical question is, "How can I avoid being spanked?"
2. **Self-Interest Orientation**. The child's critical questions are, "What's in it for me? If I do X (eat my vegetables, clean my room, go to bed on time), will I get Y (ice cream for dessert, a chance to go to a movie this weekend, the toy I want for my birthday)?"
3. **Conformity to Social Norms**. The child's critical question is, "What do good girls/boys/children do?"

4. **Maintaining Law and Order**. The adolescent's critical question is, "What will keep me from being arrested?"
5. **Participating in the Social Contract**. The young adult's critical question is, "How do civilized people behave?"
6. **Core Ethical Principles**. The adult's critical question is, "What does my conscience tell me?"

As a way of visualizing these six layers of ethical awareness, we might revise the diagram we used to illustrate the core values of an academic leader (figure 1.2) so that it now represents a more universal picture of how a person's sense of right and wrong develops (figure 4.1).

Kohlberg himself demonstrated how his stages of ethical awareness function through a scenario that has come to be known as the Heinz Dilemma.

> A woman was near death. There was one drug that the doctors thought might save her. It was a form of radium that a druggist in the same town had recently discovered. The drug was expensive to make, but the druggist was charging ten times what the drug cost him to produce. He paid $200 for the radium and charged $2,000 for a small dose of the drug. The sick woman's husband, Heinz, went to everyone he knew to borrow the money, but he could only get together about $1,000 which was half of what it cost. He told the druggist that his wife was dying and asked him to sell it cheaper or let him pay later. But the druggist said: "No, I discovered the drug and I'm going to make money from it." So Heinz got desperate and broke into the man's laboratory to steal the drug for his wife. Should Heinz have broken into the laboratory to steal the drug for his wife? Why or why not? (Kohlberg, 1981)

Kohlberg noted that the reason people gave for either approving or finding fault with Heinz's action provided insight into their stage of moral development. For example, if they believed that Heinz was wrong because he might be caught and go to prison, they were operating only on the level of maintaining law and order. The same would be true if they concluded that Heinz acted properly, but should accept his penalty as it is prescribed and reimburse the druggist when he can.

If, however, someone believed that Heinz was right to steal the drug since human life is more important than money or that Heinz was wrong because his theft may have deprived many others from access to a drug that could save them, then that person was grappling with the issue on the level of his or her core ethical values.

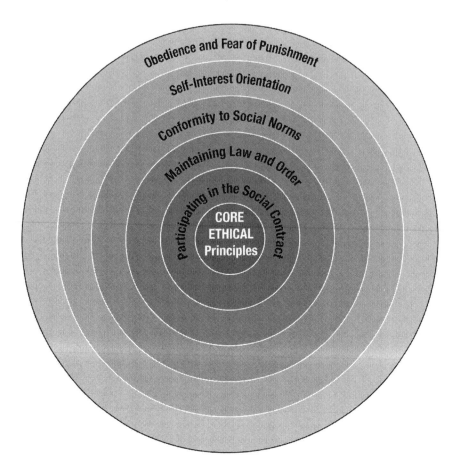

Figure 4.1.   Kohlberg's Stages of Moral Development

That last example—where we have to struggle with an ethical issue because it places two of our ethical values in conflict—provides a key to how we can determine which of our core values merits inclusion in that highly selective subset we're calling our authentic values. After all, if we rank saving someone's life ahead of our aversion to stealing, that decision tells us something significant about the values we truly believe in and that will ultimately guide our behavior.

A MODIFIED VERSION OF THE HEINZ DILEMMA

In fact, we can take this process further by updating the Heinz Dilemma and adapting it in ways to make it even more reflective of the ethical issues that concern us in higher education. Consider the following revision of the Heinz Dilemma and the questions that follow it as a way of exploring the values that you regard as most important.

> Mrs. Heinz was near death from a rare kind of cancer. There was only one drug that her doctor thought might save her. This drug was still highly experimental and had not yet earned FDA approval. Fortunately for Mrs. Heinz, the drug was developed by Dr. Hunt, a scientist at the local university.
>
> Dr. Hunt was a poor assistant professor who was still paying off a number of burdensome student loans. The initial phases of Dr. Hunt's drug research had been supported by an NIH grant, but that grant had since run out. The cancer treated by the drug was too rare for federal agencies to continue the grant, and Dr. Hunt had been forced to turn to personal resources in order to keep this research going.
>
> It cost Dr. Hunt $10,000 to make a batch of the drug, a very sizable sum in light of the loss of external funding and the professor's own financial situation. In order to continue funding this research project, Dr. Hunt had offered to provide the drug to anyone who could pay $100,000 to participate in a trial.
>
> Mr. Heinz, a disabled longshoreman who was now no longer able to work, heard about Dr. Hunt's offer and tried to raise the money. Unfortunately, Mr. Heinz only raised $20,000 from his friends and neighbors, far short of what Dr. Hunt was charging. Mr. Heinz went to see Dr. Hunt and offered $20,000 for access to the drug, arguing that this amount would at least cover the cost of making it and provide enough funding for an additional batch to continue the research.
>
> "You don't understand," Dr. Hunt replied. "This cancer is so rare that I might only sell a batch every two or three years. I have student loans to pay, living expenses to meet, and research to conduct in order to have any hope of receiving promotion and tenure. Plus there were my development costs that I already incurred. I can't consider selling you the drug for anything less than $100,000."
>
> Mr. Heinz continued to argue and plead with Dr. Hunt but to no avail. In desperation, Mr. Heinz broke into Dr. Hunt's laboratory one night and stole the drug.

QUESTIONS

1. Was Mr. Heinz wrong to do so? Why or why not?
2. Would any of the following factors cause you to change your belief about whether what Mr. Heinz did was right (or wrong)?

    a. If it could somehow be guaranteed that Mr. Heinz would never be caught and that Dr. Hunt would never suspect him.

    b. If Mrs. Heinz recovered upon receiving the drug.

    c. If the drug proved to be ineffective for Mrs. Heinz and she died anyway.

    d. If Mrs. Heinz simply received the drug too late and she died anyway.

    e. If the drug were not only ineffective in saving Mrs. Heinz but increased her suffering until she died.

3. The case study says that Mr. Heinz raised only $20,000 of the $100,000 that Dr. Hunt was charging for the new drug. It doesn't tell you anything about the Heinz's own finances. Would you change your belief about whether Mr. Heinz was right to steal the money if he and his wife had $125,000 in the bank?

    a. Suppose Mr. and Mrs. Heinz had $125,000 in the bank, but Mrs. Heinz had made Mr. Heinz swear not to touch that money because he would need it to live on due to his disability. "Even if I survive after receiving the drug," Mrs. Heinz said, "we'd both die soon because we'd have so little left to live on. Besides, I'd rather suffer than see you suffer, my dear."

    b. Suppose Mr. and Mrs. Heinz had $125,000 in the bank but Mrs. Heinz had made Mr. Heinz swear not to touch that money because he would need it to take care of their severely disabled two-year-old child whom she loved deeply.

4. Nothing in the story gives us any indication of Dr. Hunt's gender.

    a. Did you assume Dr. Hunt was a man or a woman?

    b. Why?

    c. Did that assumption in any way violate one of the core beliefs you identified in the first session of this program?

This modified version of the Heinz Dilemma provides a fictional "crucible" through which various values are set in conflict with one another.

At various points in the story and in the questions that follow it, we are asked to determine what takes precedence when we're confronted with a moral dilemma: our senses that theft is wrong, saving someone's life is important, paying off burdensome student loans might justify Dr. Hunt's action, it may be immoral to distribute a medication that has not received FDA approval, Mr. Heinz's status as a disabled longshoreman might be an extenuating circumstance in his theft, his theft is done out of love for his wife, those extenuating circumstances might be void if the Heinz family actually had substantial savings, and so on.

The sheer complexity of the modified Heinz Dilemma is both its strength and its limitation: It causes us to place a large number of values into the "crucible" simultaneously to see which emerges as most significant, but it also requires us to reflect on so many values at the same time that we may become immobilized by the number of decisions we're required to make. Fortunately, it's also possible to construct dilemmas in such a way that we don't have to weigh many different values simultaneously. We only have to consider two at a time.

TESTING OUR VALUES WITH A/B DILEMMAS

The party game "Would You Rather?" presents players with two equally attractive—or, more frequently, equally repellent—alternatives that they are forced to choose between. Examples of the type of question posed in this game are: "Would you rather that your house was designed by Dr. Seuss or M. C. Escher?" and "Would you rather have all of your hairs pulled out one by one or all of your teeth pulled out one by one?" (Gomberg and Heimberg, 2011, 582, 533).

While the object of the game is merely to amuse and sometimes embarrass the participants, this kind of either/or dilemma can be of immense value in helping us determine our hierarchy of values since it causes us to look at only two alternatives at a time.

Perhaps the most famous of the A/B Dilemmas is the so-called Trolley Problem, first articulated by Philippa Foot in 1967.

> Suppose that a judge or magistrate is faced with rioters demanding that a culprit be found for a certain crime and threatening otherwise to take their own bloody revenge on a particular section of the community. The real culprit being unknown, the judge sees himself as able to prevent the bloodshed only by framing some innocent person and having

him executed. Beside this example is placed another in which a pilot
whose airplane is about to crash is deciding whether to steer from a
more to a less inhabited area. To make the parallel as close as possible it
may rather be supposed that he is the driver of a runaway tram which
he can only steer from one narrow track on to another; five men are
working on one track and one man on the other; anyone on the track he
enters is bound to be killed. In the case of the riots the mob have five
hostages, so that in both examples the exchange is supposed to be one
man's life for the lives of five. (Foot, 1967)

In this original form of the story, readers were compelled to choose between passively allowing a situation to run its course (and thus cost the
lives of five people), or actively intervening (and thus cost the life of one
person). It set a utilitarian point of view that killing one person was
worth the net gain of four lives saved against a strict aversion to being
personally responsible for someone's murder.

But over the years, as the Trolley Problem became a common exercise
in ethics and game theory courses, it developed a number of variants:

- What would the person do if the only way to stop the runaway
  vehicle were to involve pushing an innocent person in front of it?
  This variant—a literal turn on the expression "when push comes to
  shove"—removes the mechanical intermediary of turning a steer-
  ing wheel (or in some versions, flipping a switch so as to change
  tracks) and requires the person to kill the innocent person directly.
  Many people who initially chose the utilitarian justification that the
  benefit of saving five people outweighs the evil of killing one balk
  at this alternative when they have to murder someone with their
  own hands (Thomson, 1985). Since this scenario is often presented
  as a choice about whether to push a heavy-set gentleman off a
  bridge in order to stop the trolley, it is commonly referred to as the
  "fat man" variant (Cathcart 2013; Edmonds 2015).
- What would the person do if the lone individual on the second
  track were his or her own close relative or romantic partner? This
  variant places utilitarianism in conflict with the desire to protect
  those dear to us.
- What would the person do if the five men were serial killers but the
  sole person on the other track were an award-winning pediatric
  surgeon? This variant places the utilitarian approach in conflict
  with a desire to reward good rather than evil or to view the prob-

lem from a long-term perspective: The five serial killers will probably take even more lives while the pediatric surgeon will probably save additional lives.

- What would the person do if, instead of saving people on tracks, the choice were to sacrifice one innocent and healthy organ donor to preserve the lives of five separate patients in need of vital transplants? In this variant, the utilitarian trade-off (five lives for one) is the same, but the active and intentional way in which the organ donor's basic rights are violated strikes most participants as even more singularly troubling and problematic.

- What would the person do if, instead of being confronted with a choice about saving human life, the problem were rewritten to involve preserving animal species from extinction? Ilana Ritov and Jonathan Baron (1999) developed a variant of the Trolley Problem in which participants were asked whether they'd release water from a dam in order to save twenty species of fish if doing so would cause two other species of fish further downstream to become extinct.

Many other variations also exist, involving even more ingenious ways of saving five lives at the expense of killing one person. (For the rich literature on the Trolley Problem, see Cathcart, 2013; Edmonds, 2015. For other famous A/B Dilemmas, see Vedantam, 2010, 53–54.)

The advantage of A/B Dilemmas is that they compel us to put two specific values in competition with one another and ask ourselves which one we would choose. The disadvantage of most A/B Dilemmas is that, like the Trolley Problem, they're rather artificial scenarios. We don't feel as though our authentic values are really being tested because we can't actually imagine ourselves in such contrived situations.

The solution is to experiment with A/B Dilemmas that represent situations with which we can more easily identify. For academic leaders, those situations will involve the type of ethical challenges that people do experience in higher education. For this reason, we'll next conduct another series of thought experiments in which we're asked to imagine that we are confronted with different scenarios and, in each case, given a choice between two options.

Even though the goal of the experiment is to be as realistic as possible, we do have to introduce one artificial element: You must imagine that, for whatever reason, you are being forced to choose one of the two alternatives given. You can't come up with additional options, decide that you wouldn't make either choice that you're being given, follow both alternatives, revise the scenario, or do anything other than select *either* option A *or* option B. With those restrictions in mind, consider what you'd do in each of the following situations.

1. One of your advisees comes to see you. "It looks as though I've delayed as long as I can: Today I have to declare a major and stick with it. But I need your advice. My heart's really in Field A. I love it, and I find the intellectual challenge of that discipline very exciting. But as we've discussed before, there are no jobs in that field, and my record isn't strong enough to go to graduate school in it. So, if I major in Field A, I'd end up working in some other kind of unrelated job anyway. I could also major in Field B. I really don't find it all that interesting, but I'm good at it, and there are plenty of jobs available in that field. After I graduate, I could easily get work that pays reasonably well. But I'm torn: Should I go where my heart is or where the jobs are?" You don't know anything else about this student's background or financial situation and, because your schedule is so crowded, you don't have time to ask. If you had to respond, what would you recommend to the student?

   a. "Major in the field you love and don't worry about finding a job. You'll figure it all out later."
   b. "We can't always make the choice that seems most pleasant at the time. You need to be employable when you graduate: Major in Field B."

2. Another advisee stops by. This student just needs a recommendation about what class to take next term. The same course is offered by both Dr. Smith and Dr. Jones, and the student needs to take it because it's required for her program. Dr. Smith is by far the better teacher and would provide the student with a superior academic experience. Dr. Jones is only barely adequate, covering the basic material of the course, but in a dull and uninspiring way. On the other hand, Dr. Smith is tenured, while Dr. Jones is an adjunct professor who is barely earning enough to meet expenses. Dr. Jones's courses are under-enrolled, and you know that putting this student in Dr. Jones's class will be enough to meet the dean's enrollment requirements. Without your advisee in the class, the dean

will almost certainly cancel Dr. Jones's course, leave Dr. Jones unemployed, and put his students in Dr. Smith's class. What do you do?

  a. Place the student in Dr. Smith's class. The student's interests have to come first.
  b. Place the student in Dr. Jones's class. Making sure that a colleague has a job outweighs the slight benefit that the student might get from the other course.

3. Time has gotten away from you, and you only have an hour left to prepare. If you spend it polishing your research presentation, your students will have a terrible experience in class today. If you spend it preparing for class, the research presentation you're delivering at the conference tonight will seem amateurish. How do you spend your hour?

  a. I'd prepare for class. I'm an educator, first and foremost.
  b. I'd prepare for my presentation. The students will recover from a bad class, but my career might not recover from a bad presentation.

4. Your program has conducted a faculty search for this particular position and failed so many times that your dean has told you that this is your last chance: Either you hire one of the two candidates you interviewed, or your program will lose the position and never get it back. The problem is that the two remaining candidates are so different. One is brilliant, a fine teacher and an excellent researcher, but an extraordinarily difficult colleague who would make your life at work miserable. The other is a mediocre teacher and researcher, but a really pleasant person whom you'd enjoy working with. Which candidate would you hire?

  a. The brilliant but difficult colleague.
  b. The mediocre but pleasant colleague.

5. Imagine that you're a department chair who has keys to every office in your program. Late one day, a parcel comes for one of your colleagues, and, in order to be nice, you carry it down to that person's office, unlock the door, and put the package inside. While doing so, however, you see an e-mail on the faculty member's

computer screen that makes it very clear the faculty member is having an affair with another member of the department. Even worse, the spouses of both these faculty members are also employees of the university. In fact, one of them is a close friend of yours who would be devastated by this news. You're not sure what to do, however, because your school's strong freedom of expression policy explicitly forbids supervisors from reading their employees' e-mails or other communications without permission. Which of the following would you do if they were your only choices?

    a. I would pretend that I didn't see anything. The school's policy says that I'm not supposed to read my employees' e-mails, and what people do in their personal lives is none of my business.

    b. I would have to act on what I know. I'm not sure yet whether I'd first inform the members of my department who are involved in the affair, their spouses, or all of them simultaneously. But I do know that I couldn't sit by idly with the information I had just received.

6. A few days ago, the president of your institution delivered a rather severe reprimand to a good friend of yours for missing an important deadline for a report. In anger, your friend dashed off a vicious letter to the president and sent the letter through campus mail. The following day, your friend called you, full of regret for having written such an angry letter and worried that it might lead to some very unpleasant consequences. Coincidentally, you have a meeting with the president today, and you see your friend's letter in a stack of unopened mail outside the president's office. No one is watching. What do you do?

    a. Take the letter so that the president never sees it. Your friend wrote it in anger and sincerely regrets doing so. You're just correcting your friend's mistake.

    b. Leave the letter for the president. Your friend shouldn't have written it, but you have no right to interfere.

7. Your institution has adopted a policy in which unfilled positions revert to the president and provost who can reassign them to other programs or to nonacademic units of the institution as they see fit. Due to this practice, your program has lost so many positions that you and your colleagues are finding it increasingly difficult to offer all the classes that your students need. You've just conducted a search, and, despite several rounds of interviews, you still don't have a candidate that you and others in the program feel is suitable for the position and a good fit for the department. In fact, the remaining candidates aren't just imperfect; they're absolutely awful. If the following were your only two options, which would you prefer?

   a. I'd refrain from hiring an unacceptable candidate, even though it will probably mean losing the position.
   b. I'd hire a poor candidate just to keep the position.

8. You have just started work as a tenure-track assistant professor at a new university. The institution has adopted an innovative electronic recordkeeping system for clinical services, and your own dean (who is widely known to be a difficult person) is leading the changeover. In a demonstration of the new system for about 120 students, faculty members, and staff, the dean uses an actual patient record, identifying the person's age, gender, sensitive health history, home address, and Social Security Number, among other details. You believe that the patient's privacy and personal information have been compromised, but the dean is your boss, you're untenured (and thus could lose your job with very little notice), and you feel that you're in a very vulnerable position. One day, in a meeting where you're alone with the provost, the provost asks you point blank, "Do you have any concerns about your work here this year?" Which of the following are you more likely to do?

   a. I'd not say anything about the incident mentioned above since the dean is my boss, and, while I don't agree with his decision, the decision was his to make.
   b. I'd inform the provost of my concerns about what the dean did.

9. Sarah Pennypincher is a wealthy entrepreneur who is also a patron of many philanthropic organizations. She recently joined the board of a small, local nonprofit board on which you serve as president. Pennypincher brings both substantial financial resources and an operating style that served her well in the corporate world. When decisions need to be made, Pennypincher wants orders to be issued and people to obey them. She is so overbearing that several other board members resign. To replace them, Pennypincher suggests appointing new members who worked for her in the past and seem to be willing to do whatever she wants. You've tried having a conversation with her about civility, mutual respect, the group's traditions, and board processes, but her behavior does not change. One day, another board member approaches you to say that he, as well as several more colleagues, also are increasingly upset by Pennypincher's actions and will resign unless you force her to leave the board. But doing so will cost the board a great deal financially since Pennypincher and her contacts are now the group's largest donors (by far). What do you do?

   a. I'd say that this is merely a matter of "differences in style" and maintain that, in this case, the financial ends justify the interpersonal and strategic means.
   b. I'd do whatever was necessary to remove Pennypincher from the board on the principle that the price being paid for her largesse is simply too high.

10. For some time now, you've been concerned over actions taken by Mustafa, a business manager your university hired to assist with the very complex cooperative programs you conduct with several major firms in the region. When a consultant was needed on a project, the person Mustafa hired (at a rather high fee) was later rumored to be a close friend of Mustafa. You've also been suspicious of several expenditures Mustafa approved that, in your opinion, were too high for the services that were provided; the rumors you heard were that, once again, Mustafa approved them primarily to benefit his friends and family. At first, you assumed that these rumors were, like most rumors, simply the matter of idle gossip. Certainly on those occasions when you questioned one of Mustafa's actions, he replied that it was just an unintentional error and

took steps to correct it. But now these "errors" seem to have become so numerous that you're beginning to wonder whether the rumors are true. Nevertheless, you don't have any real evidence that Mustafa did anything wrong intentionally. What do you decide to do?

    a. Take steps to have Mustafa fired. Even though the evidence is not conclusive, your suspicions alone are reasons to want a new business manager. If it later turns out that Mustafa was doing something wrong, you'll be held accountable as his supervisor. It's better not to take chances.

    b. Insist that Mustafa be mentored and that his work be supervised by another business manager. After all, you don't have any real proof that Mustafa has done anything wrong, and it would be a terrible thing to dismiss someone who may well have been guilty of nothing more than an honest mistake.

11. You are the chair of a search committee that is charged with hiring the director of an innovative new academic program. Your good friend Lewis has applied for that position, and you very much want him to get the job. You think Lewis will be excellent in this position, and you look forward to having this new program headed by someone you like so much. It's now a few days before the rest of the search committee will begin reviewing the applications. You're getting materials organized, and you notice that Lewis's application is far less well-prepared than those of the other applicants. Maybe he was lazy. Maybe he assumed your friendship was all he needed to get the job. Or maybe he just underestimated the level of detail required. In any case, his résumé is not very detailed, and his cover letter is filled with typographical errors. He also failed to provide a list of references, as specified in the search announcement. At the outset of the search, you felt you could be objective in the process and would avoid giving Lewis an unfair advantage. But now you realize that, unless you do something, Lewis will probably be overlooked by the rest of the search committee. What do you do?

a. Alert Lewis to the problem and have him resubmit a better set of application materials.

b. Let Lewis take his chances with the search committee: It is his own fault if his materials were poorly prepared.

12. A political science professor has very strong opinions about a recent election in your state. He believes that the person who was elected to be governor is unfit for office, an advocate of disastrous economic policies, and successful in the election only because of deceitful and possibly illegal practices. This political science professor is about to enter an auditorium where he intends to deliver a public lecture denouncing the governor and recommending that the state immediately begin a recall election. As the two of you are chatting before the lecture, the head of security comes up and announces that there's a report that an angry, possibly psychotic supporter of the governor has been seen in the audience. This particular supporter is believed to be dangerous and has threatened to attack or even kill anyone who speaks out against the governor. As it happens, you live in a state that permits citizens to carry concealed weapons on college campuses, even at large public meetings. The head of security says that they'll do what they can to protect the speaker but, in such a crowded venue, they can't absolutely guarantee his safety. The professor asks you which of the following he should do.

a. Assert his academic freedom, speak his mind, and take his chances.

b. Tone down his remarks greatly, despite his convictions, in order to avoid aggravating a potential assailant.

DRAWING CONCLUSIONS FROM THE A/B DILEMMAS

As with our exercise involving the Krathwohl Taxonomy, it would be best if we could create A/B Dilemmas for all the principles you included among your core values to determine which of them truly stand as authentic values for you. But, since it's impossible to know which values you selected, the dilemmas that we just considered were created from the values people have repeatedly told me in workshops over the years and that were among the most significant for them. If you look back at the twelve dilemmas you just considered, you'll see that the conflicts you had to struggle with were the following:

1. Holistic orientation versus vocational orientation;
2. Student-centeredness versus faculty orientation;
3. Teaching-first orientation versus research orientation;
4. Brilliance versus collegiality;
5. Chain of command (or confidentiality/discretion) versus transparency;
6. Friendship versus objectivity;
7. Pursuit of excellence versus discipline/field orientation;
8. Chain of command versus confidentiality/discretion;
9. Discipline/field orientation (or thrift) versus collegiality;
10. Accountability versus trust;
11. Friendship versus honesty;
12. Academic freedom versus practicality (at least in the form of a desire for self-preservation).

If you want to test your level of commitment to values that don't appear on this list, you can also create your own A/B Dilemmas. You simply imagine as realistic a situation as possible in which you would be forced to choose between two values that you regard as equally important to you.

For example, let's suppose that you believe you have the same level of dedication to both integrity and shared governance. What might be a situation that would bring those two values into conflict? Perhaps you can imagine a scenario in which you're a department chair who pledged your word that, if the dean would permit you to bring a fourth candidate to campus for an interview in a search with a particularly large pool of qualified applicants, you would respect his or her decision about which finalist to hire.

That pledge made sense at the time because all four candidates you were recommending looked equally good on paper and did extremely well in their phone interviews. And indeed, now that the four candidates have all visited campus, you yourself still have no preferences among them.

But the search committee and other members of your program strongly favor a different candidate from the one whom the dean told you privately he or she wants to hire. Do you honor your commitment to respect the dean's choice, or does your commitment to shared government impel you to try making the case for the others in your program? The goal is to create a scenario that backs you into a corner: If you act in accordance with one of your values, you have to violate the other.

You can also gain experience in dealing with ethical challenges of this kind by participating in Harvard University's Moral Sense Test (Henry, 2015). There are a number of surveys included in this test (such as one examining whether the participant has psychopathic traits and another examining how the participant thinks about difficult actions), but the survey most relevant to our current discussion is the Web site's Morality Questionnaire.

In this online exercise, participants are confronted with a number of difficult choices (including the Trolley Problem) that are actually A/B Dilemmas in disguise. Then the participant is asked to use a sliding scale to indicate whether the choice stated in the story is forbidden, permissible, obligatory, or at some point between those options.

At the end of the survey, the participant's responses are ranked against others who have participated in the study, with insight provided into whether his or her responses tended to be utilitarian in nature (the greatest good for the greatest number of people), deontological in nature (certain matters are universally right or wrong regardless of circumstances), or somewhere in between.

Like the Trolley Problem, the other scenarios outlined in the Moral Sense Test tend to be artificial and (some might argue) farfetched. Nevertheless, as Thomas Cathcart has argued, "such thought experiments, by their very simplicity, can help us clarify the way we make—or should make—more complicated ethical decisions" (Cathcart, 2013, 5).

Although the A/B Dilemmas that we've been exploring have served as an exercise in testing your commitment to your authentic values, there are also situations in which real-life A/B Dilemmas do occur.

One instance involved the City College of San Francisco, where a group of trustees proposed curricular changes to remedial English and math courses in an effort to improve the rate at which black and Latino students were able to proceed to college-level courses in a timely manner.

"There's been a fair amount of contention about the process here," said Karen Saginor, president of the Academic Senate and a tenured librarian at the college. "Under state law, any curricular decisions have to be made by faculty. The normal process is that the departments that are affected write proposals. In this case, a couple of trustees wrote a resolution saying that the curriculum will be like this, and that was just not really the way to do it." Still, many faculty members are sympathetic to the argument that the remedial track, especially in English and math, takes way too long to complete, leading many students to leave college before reaching college courses. Faculty would just have preferred to bring forth concerns about it themselves. (Moltz, 2010)

In this case, the values in conflict were faculty orientation (particularly in the area of curriculum) and commitment to diversity. Academic professionals who believe that the principle of faculty control of the curriculum outweighs the potential benefits of the new proposals would resist them. Those who believe that anything that might benefit minority students should be attempted, regardless of who proposed the idea, would support them.

As is so often the case in actual situations, there were attempts to find common ground and seek a compromise solution, but the very fact that the dilemma arose in the first place illustrates that conflicts between two ethical principles do arise in the workplace. In fact, they may be particularly common in higher education where administrators and faculty members have such strong commitments to values arising from their disciplines, creating the possibility that their personal values, social values, and professional values may at times be at odds with one another.

On a much smaller scale, academic leaders encounter a real-life A/B Dilemma every time they receive reference calls about a colleague who has a long history of being difficult or uncivil. Do they help their current programs by giving this person a glowing reference in the hope that he or she will be hired somewhere else or do they provide an honest appraisal, knowing that their own programs will continue to suffer because of their difficult colleague's behavior?

If the academic leaders were asked whether they valued honesty and helping their programs thrive, they'd probably respond that both of these qualities are very important to them. But in actual situations in which a choice has to be made between a candid response and a response that's in the best interest of the academic leaders' current programs, one of these values has to be given precedence over the other.

Another common situation in which a real-life A/B Dilemma occurs is when academic leaders learn confidential information that they have promised to protect, but also have a professional duty to inform others about the content of this privileged information.

Students commonly approach faculty members and initiate conversations by saying, "I need to tell you something. But I don't want you to report it to anyone or to do anything about it." The best response in such a situation is to stop the student, before he or she says anything more, and note that, depending on what he or she says, you may be professionally *required* to report that information to others.

Sometimes, however, the student blurts out the confidential information before you have a chance to issue a warning. In such a case, Linda Taylor and Howard Adelman provide a useful script for how to respond:

> Although most of what we talk about is private, there are three kinds of problems you might tell me about that we would have to talk about with other people. If I find out that someone has been seriously hurting or abusing you, I would have to tell the authorities about it. If you tell me you have made a plan to seriously hurt yourself, I would have to let your parents know. If you tell me you have made a plan to seriously hurt someone else, I would have to warn that person. I would not be able to keep these problems just between you and me because the law says I can't. Do you understand that it's okay to talk about everything and there are only three things we must talk about with other people? (Taylor and Adelman, 1998, 272)

Such language does not, of course, resolve the dilemma, but it does provide you with a workable plan for moving forward.

RESOLVING A/B DILEMMAS

Are there then any ways to resolve an A/B Dilemma (either actual or hypothetical) when just examining the values in question and deciding which one matters more to us is not enough? In other words, can we resolve a moral dilemma when, despite our best efforts, we still find ourselves at an impasse?

One practical approach to resolving moral dilemmas is the **Kidder Paradigm**, developed by Rushworth Kidder (1944–2012), founder of the Institute for Moral Ethics. As presented in such books as *How Good People Make Tough Choices* (2003) and *Moral Choices* (2005), the Kidder Paradigm consists of nine steps, but it's easier to understand if we group these steps into three sections.

I. The Knowledge Section. What do I need to know in order to increase the likelihood that I will be able to resolve this dilemma?

Step 1. Does an ethical dilemma genuinely exist? In other words, is this really a conflict among my core values, or are matters of personal preference, manners, aesthetics, social convention, or simply the everyday challenges of life complicating my view? For example, a parent may feel torn between wanting a child to develop confidence by supporting his or her right to make decisions and believing that the child's choice of dress is wholly inappropriate and likely to cause teachers and prospective employers to assume that the child is immoral or disrespectful. The parent has to decide whether the issue is truly a choice between competing values (such as trust versus morality) or between a value and a matter of personal taste or preference.

Step 2. Whose dilemma is it? Is this moral challenge actually mine as an *actor*, or am I really just an observer? Am I *responsible* for what happens? For example, someone may feel conflicted about wanting to be supportive of a friend and believing that he or she is in a romantic relationship that will end in heartbreak. The question this person has to decide is whether it is even appropriate to become actively involved in making this choice or if it is a matter better left for his or her friend to resolve.

Step 3. What are the indisputable facts? What do I know for certain versus what am I assuming? How might my own preconceived notions or past history be influencing my view of the situation? For example, a person may want to begin a new romantic relationship, but be hesitant because his or her last few romantic partners all proved to be disloyal. The question this person needs to decide is whether his or her past history is distorting how the present situation may be seen. A past lover's infidelity has no effect at all on the reliability of a potential lover. At the same time, if similar scenarios have been repeated often enough, the person may be right to wonder whether he or she tends to be attracted to self-destructive relationships, for whatever reason.

II: The Test Section. Now that I have the knowledge I need, what touchstones can I apply to the dilemma to help me determine how I should proceed?

Step 4. Right-versus-Wrong Tests:

    a. *The legal test:* Is one or more of the options I'm considering against the law?

    b. *The intuition test:* Does something about one or more of my options "smell wrong" or seem "off"? Does an option make me feel uncomfortable in a way that makes me question its suitability as a course of action I should take?

    c. *The publicity test:* How would I feel if others read about what I had decided on the front page of the local newspaper or in the *Chronicle of Higher Education*? Would one of my options embarrass me more than my other possible choices?

    d. *The moral exemplar test:* How would I feel if my parent/spouse/boss/mentor/best friend found out that I had chosen a particular option? Would I be ashamed to have taken any of the choices that I'm considering?

Step 5. The Four Dilemmas Test: As I consider the issue I'm trying to resolve, on which side of these four dilemmas does each choice fall? In light of my values, would I be comfortable with my actions being on that particular side of the dilemma in question?

    a. *Truth versus Loyalty.* This particular dilemma in the Kidder Paradigm generally causes confusion and misunderstanding. So, it seems best to rephrase it as Transparency versus Confidentiality. Recall our earlier scenario in which a student tells you something in confidence that you feel morally or professionally obliged to report. Which side do you feel you must favor: truth and transparency or loyalty and confidentiality?

    b. *Short-Term Benefits versus Long-Term Benefits.* Which is motivating me most in the current situation: my immediate needs, comfort, and preferences or my enduring welfare, or the urgency of a pressing crisis or the desire to invest in a better future?

    c. *Justice versus Mercy.* Do this situation and the history that produced it suggest that the current dilemma is better addressed through the impartial assignment of rewards and sanctions or through compassion, generosity, and forbearance?

    d. *Self versus Community.* Is this a time when I should be standing up for myself or acting on behalf of others? Who is more likely to be taken advantage of or victimized: myself or others?

Step 6. The Resolution Principles: Three time-tested approaches to resolving moral dilemmas. Not all of these principles may be applicable to each situation, but one or more of them will often provide guidance as to which choice may be more ethically defended and why.

    a. *Kantian, the moral imperative:* What would happen if each option I am considering became a universal rule that everyone in the world would then have to follow?

    b. *Utilitarian:* Which option would result in the greatest good for the largest number of people?

    c. *The Golden Rule:* Am I treating others as I would want to be treated in a similar situation?

III: The Decision Section

Step 7. Avoid alternative blindness. Sometimes, by seeing a moral situation as a choice between A and B, I may be blinding myself to the fact that other possibilities exist. With this idea in mind, do I have another option? Is compromise possible? Could I simply choose not to choose?

Step 8. Avoid decision paralysis. After going through the first seven steps carefully and conscientiously, it's time to make the decision. Realizing that I can't know the future and will never have all the information I might desire, I have to make the decision on the basis of the best insight I have right now and the ethical principles that I regard as most important. Unless this situation is one that calls for intentional inaction on my part, I have to realize that failure to do anything could easily result in consequences more undesirable than either choice before me.

There comes a time in every reflective process to act, and I have now reached it.

Step 9. Reflect on the decision. After the choice has been made, I have to deal with and learn from the consequences of my decision. Would I do the same thing again if I could go back and revisit my decision? What did I learn about myself and my core values from this process? If I conclude that the choice I made was a mistake, how can I repair the damage or make amends?

The great advantage that the Kidder Paradigm has over other systems for resolving moral dilemmas is that it is systematic and comprehensive. In the emotionally tumultuous environment in which many ethical dilemmas have to be solved, we may feel under such pressure that we panic and skip steps that would have helped us reach a more satisfactory solution. We are tempted to be more product-oriented or process-oriented than principle-oriented, and thus we may end up making decisions that we come to regret later.

But by helping us move progressively through these nine steps—from finding out the key details we need in order to make our decision, to guiding us through tests that help us see the dilemma more objectively, and then to forcing us to make a decision—the Kidder Paradigm prevents us from skipping over crucial components in any values-based process. Moreover, it does not assume that any one values system or resolution principle will provide us with every answer to every challenge. It is, in other words, a framework that we can use to test and apply our own authentic values.

If there were any of the hypothetical A/B Dilemmas presented earlier in this chapter that caused you particular difficulty or that you were unable to resolve at all, go back to them now, and use the Kidder Paradigm to see whether it makes your choice any clearer. Moreover, if you need to rethink the priority order by which you have ranked your authentic values, this paradigm can be a valuable tool in confirming or modifying your commitment to different principles.

QUANDARIES AND PREDICAMENTS

A/B Dilemmas are both real in terms of the challenges that academic leaders actually face and, as hypothetical exercises, techniques we can use to measure our commitment to one value over another.

Yet many of the challenges we face as academic leaders don't fall into this neat A/B division. They're thus a little bit more like the Heinz Dilemma than the Trolley Problem in that they offer us many different possibilities to choose from or, in the most troubling scenarios we might encounter, no scenarios at all. For the sake of reference, we will designate an ethical challenge of particular complexity with numerous possible choices as a **quandary** and an ethical challenge with no apparent solution as a **predicament**.

Quandaries are more common than predicaments. As academic leaders, we're likely to encounter a quandary of at least a minor sort several times a semester. Situations arise where any given choice we make might benefit the students, the faculty, the administration, our institution, or our academic discipline while failing to benefit (or even causing harm to) one or more of the other stakeholders that we're considering.

Fortunately, the Kidder Paradigm can be just as useful in helping us analyze quandaries as it is with dilemmas. Its nine steps enable us to distinguish the most relevant factors from issues that may seem pressing at the time, but are ultimately insignificant.

Unfortunately, since predicaments by definition have no solution—at least, they lack a solution that we can determine at the moment we need one—they are less easily addressed through the Kidder Paradigm. Nevertheless, predicaments can prove to be the greatest tests of our authentic values and represent those situations where our principle-oriented motivation is most needed.

The predicaments that keep us awake at night wondering if we did the right thing and how matters would have turned out if we had decided differently tend to be those that deal with the big questions in life. We find ourselves called on to make a decision that affects someone's livelihood, career, and sense of self-worth, and there's no outcome we can think of that doesn't cause harm to others and can't backfire once our decision's been made. Even worse, if we're ever called on to serve on a jury or to intervene in a violent situation, our actions can literally mean the difference between life and death to someone, perhaps even to a number of people.

While these situations are the most troubling, they're also the most complex, and each situation is likely to be unique to us at a particular moment in time, involving a particular group of people and particular circumstances that won't ever apply again to us (and certainly never apply to anyone else reading this book). So, rather than explore one of these extremely serious and life-changing predicaments, I'd like to close this chapter by examining a far humbler scenario, one that I'll call the **Buller Predicament** because it actually happened to me.

One day I needed to mail several packages and also buy some stamps at the post office. It was late in the evening, so the main part of the post office was closed, but the lobby contained several self-service machines that could take care of everything I wanted to do. It was shortly before a holiday, and I wasn't the only person who had this idea: The lines at each machine were long, and I waited nearly twenty minutes before my turn arrived.

I weighed each package in turn, printed the stamps that I needed, and proceeded to check out. The total came to just over $200, which seemed quite a lot for my packages and stamps, but shipping often costs more than I expect, and I thought, "Maybe that's right." I got out my credit card and was preparing to pay when suddenly the screen on the machine said, "Thank you! Come again!" and reset for the next customer's use.

I was confused. I hadn't even put my credit card into the machine, and yet the transaction was over. I was staring at the machine in confusion for several moments (probably irritating those who were waiting in line behind me) when I suddenly realized what had happened: The person in front of me in line had never completed his or her transaction.

That person must have gotten to the point of inserting a credit card but hadn't proceeded all the way to the final screen. When I stepped up with my packages, the postal machine simply acted as though I were the last person adding a few more items to that purchase and tacked my stamps and packages onto his or her charges.

I printed out the receipt. For security reasons, the person's credit card information didn't appear. In fact, there was absolutely no indication of who the person was. Focusing on my own business, I hadn't even paid attention to what the person ahead of me looked like or whether it was a man or a woman. I immediately went to the parking lot to see if I could spot anyone. In the several minutes it took me to weigh my packages and buy my stamps, the person had left.

The next day, I returned to the post office during business hours and asked whether there was any way they could determine who that anonymous customer had been. They assured me that they had no way of doing so, and I was thus left with the following predicament:

- What's the proper course of action to take when you've just inadvertently stolen over $100 from a stranger and have no way of finding out who that person was?
- Since it was an accident but involved a situation that seemed so contrary to what I regarded as my authentic values, how should I feel about what had happened? What, if anything, should I learn from it?
- What was the most ethical action I could take moving forward?

When I present this predicament in workshops on values-based leadership, the suggestions that people have are tremendously varied:

- Don't do anything, and don't feel bad. It was an accident, and accidents happen.
- Go back to the post office. Leave your telephone number and a brief account of what happened. If no one contacts the post office and reports the loss within a year, consider the matter closed.
- Pay it forward: Donate to charity the same amount of money you inadvertently charged to the other person's credit card.
- Pay it forward: Offer to pay for someone else's packages and stamps sometime in the future.

The variety of these suggestions—and often the confidence people have in making them—made it clear to me that predicaments are useful windows into someone's authentic values and how that person approaches morally ambiguous situations.

For example, the suggestion that some people made, urging me merely to get over any sense of guilt because what had happened was just an accident, suggests that these people saw responsibility as significantly related to intentionality. If a person isn't consciously trying to do something improper or to harm someone else, then his or her responsibility to rectify the situation has limits.

They were likely to conclude that academic leaders who launched an initiative that ended up wasting much needed resources or causing a great deal of damage could be excused because they were, after all, just *trying* to help. It's a fair question to wonder whether those who had to repair the damage or live with the results of those bad decisions felt the same after those academic leaders went on to higher administrative positions at other institutions.

The identification of responsibility with intentionality also lies behind the advice that some people gave to leave my name as contact information at the post office in the hope that the injured party might return to inquire about the additional charges on his or her credit card. According to this perspective, as long as I made an effort to make amends (which was often presented with a statute of limitations of a year or so), I had met my moral responsibility. Anything further would be unnecessarily and, at least in the opinion of some people, ridiculously excessive.

On the other hand, those who believed I had an obligation to make some recompense for my unintentional theft by paying it forward in some way seemed to be drawing a firm line between intentionality and responsibility. Regardless of whether I had wanted to have the other postal customer charged for my purchases, he or she ended up paying for them. As a result, I had an obligation to do *something* willingly benefiting another person to the same extent that I had unwillingly harmed the person in front of me in line.

The final opinion—and the one that I personally find the most interesting—suggests that this particular victim deserved to be victimized: He or she hadn't completed the transaction properly and so was responsible for the accidental overcharge.

When I'm presented with this point of view in workshops, I like to ask a follow-up question: Would the person feel the same way if my action had not been accidental? In other words, suppose I had been a devious person, observed that the last customer left before completing his or her transaction, and thought, "What a fool! I'm going to add my purchases to that person's charge. In fact, I think I'll get even more stamps than I'd intended." Would the person still feel that the customer deserved to be treated that way?

In the workshops I've conducted, an overwhelming majority of people then change their opinion. If I intentionally steal from the other customer, then the fault becomes mine. (The assumption, in such a case, appears to be that there's only one set of blame to be assigned in each scenario; if I'm innocent, the other person must be responsible, but, if I act intentionally, he or she becomes absolved of responsibility.)

The remaining 10 percent to 20 percent of participants in this mental experiment stick to their guns: Since the first customer committed the error of not finalizing the transaction, he or she deserved whatever happened, even if I intentionally took advantage of the situation.

If that perspective seems heartless, we have to remember that we do often encounter it in daily life. There are plenty of people who conclude that a scantily clad young woman was "asking for it" when she was sexually assaulted or that victims of identity theft "got what they deserved" by not being careful enough when clicking on links in e-mail messages.

As we'll see in the next chapter, my purpose in discussing these issues with academic leaders isn't to praise or condemn any particular ethical conclusion—I'll leave it to those who write about leadership virtues to do that—but rather to help people understand what their authentic values truly are. It can sometimes be rather humbling to realize that, even though you may view yourself as a highly ethical person, the choices you make in various situations may not always leave you in the company of the saints.

To my mind, that's the great value of ethical predicaments when they arise: They become the moral equivalent of Rorschach inkblots onto which we project our own authentic values because the situations don't lend themselves to clear and unambiguous solutions.

Like A/B Dilemmas and quandaries, predicaments also occur in real life. Academic leaders have to decide how they will handle situations in which they help a student work through a problem, provide the best advice they can, and then discover that the student committed suicide that night. Does the academic leader feel responsible at least to some degree? *Should* the academic leader feel responsible? In either case, what's the best way for the academic leader to handle similar situations in the future?

Or, a protégé comes to a mentor wanting to pursue Project A, but the mentor persuades the protégé that Project B is better. If that advice ends up being wrong and the protégé would have graduated, received tenure, or been hired if he or she had actually done Project B, how should the mentor respond? To what extent are advisors responsible for the content and quality of the advice they give, and to what extent are people responsible for choosing to follow that advice (even if it would have been extremely difficult to have gone against the recommendations of a powerful advisor)?

The goal of authentic academic leadership isn't to eliminate these predicaments. No leadership approach can do that. Our goal instead is to discover what our authentic values are so that we better handle the dilemmas, quandaries, and predicaments that will inevitably come our way. Moreover, it is to enable us to act in ways that will benefit our stakeholders, academic programs, and institutions even if we happen to embrace a set of values that others may question or reject.

In order to understand how we can do so, we need first to return to an issue first raised at the beginning of this book, and that's the task that will occupy us in the next chapter.

KEY POINTS FROM CHAPTER 4

- In explorations of values-based leadership, the term *crucible* is often used to describe a difficult situation that tests a person's commitment to his or her core values.
- Kohlberg Dilemmas are hypothetical situations that are used to determine at what stage of moral development someone is according to a theory developed by Lawrence Kohlberg.
- A/B Dilemmas take two values a person says he or she claims to support, place those values in conflict with one another, and compel the person to choose between the two values.
- The Kidder Paradigm is a useful procedure for helping people resolve moral dilemmas.
- Quandaries are ethical challenges that confront us with multiple options from which we have to choose the best from among several good choices or the least bad from among several poor choices.
- Predicaments are ethical challenges that seem to have no satisfactory solution at all. By forcing us to invent a course of action (even if that course of action isn't really a solution), predicaments are particularly good opportunities for us to discover our authentic values.

REFERENCES

Bennis, W. G., & Thomas, R. J. (2002). *Geeks & geezers: How era, values, and defining moments shape leaders.* Boston: Harvard Business School Press.

Cathcart, T. (2013). *The trolley problem: Or would you throw the fat man off the bridge?: A philosophical conundrum.* New York: Workman.

Edmonds, D. (2015). *Would you kill the fat man?: The trolley problem and what your answer tells us about right and wrong.* Princeton, NJ: Princeton University Press.

Foot, P. (1967). The problem of abortion and the doctrine of the double effect in virtues and vices. *Oxford Review. 5*, 5–15.

George, B. (2003). *Authentic leadership: Rediscovering the secrets to creating lasting value.* San Francisco: Jossey-Bass.

Gomberg, D., & Heimberg, J. (2011). *Would you rather?: An absolutely absurd anthology.* New York: Seven Footer Press.

Henry, M. (2015). The moral sense test. http://www.moralsensetest.com.

Kidder, R. M. (2003). *How good people make tough choices: Resolving the dilemmas of ethical living.* New York: Quill.

Kidder, R. M. (2005). *Moral courage: Ethics in action.* Camden, ME: Institute for Global Ethics.

Kohlberg, L. (1981). *Essays on moral development, vol. I: The philosophy of moral development.* San Francisco: Harper & Row.

Moltz, D. (June 28, 2010). Competing principles. *Inside Higher Ed.* https://www.insidehighered.com/news/2010/06/28/remediation.

Ritov, I., & Baron, J. (1999). Protected values and omission bias. *Organizational Behavior and Human Decision Processes. 79*(2), 79–94.

Shugart, S. (2013). *Leadership in the crucible of work: Discovering the interior life of an authentic leader.* Maitland, FL: Florida Hospital Publishing.

Smith, A. M. (2013). *A conspiracy of friends.* New York: Anchor Books.

Taylor, L., & Adelman, H. S. (1998). Confidentiality: Competing principles, inevitable dilemmas. *Journal of Educational and Psychological Consultation. 9*(3), 267–76.

Thomas, R. J. (2008). *Crucibles of leadership: How to learn from experience to become a great leader.* Boston: Harvard Business School Press.

Thomson, J. J. (May 1985). The trolley problem. *Yale Law Journal. 94*(6), 1395–415.

Vedantam, S. (2010). *The hidden brain: How our unconscious minds elect presidents, control markets, wage wars, and save our lives.* New York: Spiegel & Grau.

RESOURCES

Bartels, D. M., Bauman, C. W., Cushman, F. A., Pizarro, D. A., & McGraw, A. P. (2015). Moral judgment and decision making. In Keren, G., & Wu, G. *The Wiley Blackwell handbook of judgment and decision making.* Malden, MA. 478–515.

Bauman, C. W., McGraw, A. P., Bartels, D. M., & Warren, C. (2014). Revisiting external validity: Concerns about trolley problems and other sacrificial dilemmas in moral psychology. *Social and Personality Psychology Compass. 8,* 536–54.

Broeders, R., van den Bos, K., Muller, P. A., & Ham, J. (2011). Should I save or should I not kill? How people solve moral dilemmas depends on which rule is most accessible. *Journal of Experimental Social Psychology. 47,* 923–34.

Lombrozo, T. (2009). The role of moral commitments in moral judgment. *Cognitive Science. 33,* 273–86.

Nichols, S., & Mallon, R. (2006). Moral dilemmas and moral rules. *Cognition. 100*(3), 530–42.

Paharia, N., Kassam, K. S., Greene, J. D., & Bazerman, M. H. (2009). Dirty work, clean hands: The moral psychology of indirect agency. *Organizational Behavior and Human Decision Processes. 109,* 134–41.

Part III

The Paradox of Authenticity

FIVE

What's So Good about Being Bad?

Progress isn't made by early risers. It's made by lazy men trying to find easier ways to do something.

—Robert A. Heinlein (1988) 53

In chapter 1, we encountered a problem that I called the *paradox of authenticity*, which may be summarized as follows: authentic leadership (whether academic or otherwise) means being true to one's own values and using those values to guide one's decisions and actions as a leader; but what is a person to do if his or her values are socially unacceptable or, as the proponents of virtue-based leadership would have it, morally wrong?

Is it better to "fake it 'til you make it"—as the adage popular in twelve-step programs and elsewhere would have it—or to be an honest and open reprobate? And if the better option turns out to be acting virtuously despite one's true beliefs and inclinations, how in the world can we claim that we're being *authentic*?

Most books that advocate authentic leadership ignore this paradox. They assume that values-based leadership and authentic leadership are identical. In fact, they go even further by prescribing what an authentic leader's values should be.

Thus Robert Terry believes that authentic leaders are inclined to "do the right thing" (whatever that might be); Bill George concludes that authentic leaders will act with compassion, self-discipline, and trust in others; and Fred Walumbwa, Bruce Avolio, and others posit that authentic leaders are confident, optimistic, and transparent in their relations

(Terry and Cleveland, 1993, 68, 251; George, 2003, 18–43; and Walumbwa, Peterson, Avolio, Wernsing, and Gardner, 2008, 94).

But suppose you conducted the thought experiments and reflections outlined in the previous chapters and concluded that you're a callous, undisciplined, distrustful, insecure, pessimistic, and guarded academic leader who's constantly tempted to do the *wrong* thing.

Is authentic academic leadership just not for you? And if so, what are we to make of the other discovery we made in chapter 1, that hypocrisy— even if (or perhaps *especially if*) it means pretending to have a virtue that one actually lacks—irreparably undermines a leader's ability to be effective in embodying other values or virtues? Is the leader then condemned to failure regardless of whether he or she imitates socially acceptable values or authentically embodies socially unacceptable ones?

Near the end of the 1939 film *The Wizard of* Oz, the title character responds to Dorothy's accusation that he's a very bad man with the words, "Oh, no, my dear. I'm a very good man. I'm just a very bad wizard" (LeRoy and Fleming, 1939). Is it possible to reverse this formula and be a very bad man (or woman), but a very good dean? As an initial step toward answering all the questions we've just raised, let's conduct another thought experiment, this time involving an academic leader whom we'll call Dean Vader.

THOUGHT EXPERIMENT: DEAN VADER

Imagine the following scenario: Few people would characterize Dean Vader as a good person, at least in a conventional way. He may not rise to Dorothy's standards for "a very bad man," but he does seem to care mostly about his career, which to him means becoming provost as quickly as possible as a stepping-stone to becoming a university president.

He is terribly impatient, has an inflated ego, doesn't like to work particularly hard, and loves to hear himself praised in as lavish detail as possible. He's certainly not generous; he hardly gives any money to charity, preferring to spend money on expensive suits and luxury automobiles. Some would even call him a snob.

And yet, almost everyone seems to be in agreement that Dean Vader has been a pretty good dean. It seems a paradox. Shouldn't people's excellence in leadership derive from their virtues or at least their more positive qualities? How might it be possible Dean Vader's *less* agreeable qualities as a person actually make him rather successful as an academic leader? How might authentic academic leadership actually be better for both Dean Vader and his college than pretending to be someone he's not?

As a means of answering these questions, we might begin by realizing that negative characteristics, socially unacceptable qualities, and character flaws can sometimes become the impetus for positive change. In Laurel Thatcher Ulrich's commonly quoted (and even more commonly misquoted and misattributed) phrase, "Well-behaved women seldom make history" (Ulrich, 1976, 20).

Or as screenwriters Stanley Weiser and Oliver Stone have the character Gordon Gekko say in the 1987 film *Wall Street*, "greed—for lack of a better word—is good. Greed is right. Greed works. Greed clarifies, cuts through, and captures the essence of the evolutionary spirit. Greed, in all of its forms— greed for life, for money, for love, knowledge—has marked the upward surge of mankind" (Pressman and Stone, 1987).

We may be repelled by the values that Gekko represents and recall his ultimate fate in the movie (before his partial redemption in the 2010 sequel), but recognize the truth of his observation: Greed has been known to prompt people toward actions that ultimately benefited their families, communities, and humanity as a whole. In fact, the entire capitalist system is based on the concept of enlightened self-interest, which essentially means that the interest of the individual and the interest of the public are tightly interrelated.

We can cite numerous similar examples:

- Obsessive people can be dogged in their determination to achieve goals or complete tasks.
- Confrontational people can challenge others to defend their positions in ways that end up strengthening their beliefs and providing clarity to their convictions.
- Envious people can bring about a leap of improvement because they're dissatisfied with the state of their own programs when comparing them to others.
- Cold, calculating people can identify rational solutions that others may hesitate to voice for fear of offending or inconveniencing those they care about.
- Cowardly people provide a voice of caution when others might charge headlong into risky situations.

- Impulsive people can sometimes generate spontaneous, creative ideas that would never have occurred to their more cautious colleagues.
- Unpredictable people can keep others on their toes and thus help avoid complacency.
- People who quit when success would require unreasonable investment of money, time, or effort can often save valuable resources, and, at times, even people's lives regardless of the fact that we often glamorize those who persevere despite long odds (Kashdan and Biswas-Diener, 2014, 15–17).
- Narcissists may be able to achieve ambitious goals largely because they believe so strongly in themselves. As Todd Kashdan and Robert Biswas-Diener conclude:

> Narcissists with their huge egos and sense of entitlement often take on projects that intimidate others. While many of those projects fail, they have enough confidence in their own talents that they continue trying until they're eventually successful. Rather than fantasizing about hosting a television show, for instance, narcissists are more likely to go out and try to do just that. The confidence of people who lean toward self-absorption derives from a sense of specialness. It's entirely possible that a feeling of uniqueness and a dollop of entitlement gave us the iPhone, the Human Genome Project, Microsoft Windows, an independent Israeli state, the Oprah Book Club, and *Exile on Main Street*. (Kashdan and Biswas-Diener, 2014, 161)

And we can do something similar with opinions or perspectives that are likely to be unpopular with many people in the academic world.

For example, a professor who has a very low opinion of undergraduates and sees them primarily as obstacles to his or her own research may end up raising the bar for students and challenging them intellectually in a way that more supportive, nurturing faculty members do not. A dean or department chair that is inaccessible and spends a great deal of time away from campus might develop a level of independence and initiative among the faculty that other administrators would envy.

You can probably add many other examples to this list. The point is that good outcomes don't only result from our virtues and socially admired values. They can also result from our vices, unpopular opinions, and character flaws.

And having positive outcomes flow from negative or at least questionable impulses certainly seems to have been the case for our hypothetical administrator, Dean Vader. We may be annoyed by résumé builders like Dean Vader and feel that we're being used by them mostly to further their own careers, but self-aggrandizers can bring about circumstances that benefit others.

In wanting to have a record of spectacular achievements for others to admire, they often make sure that their achievements are truly spectacular. Although they may take credit for everything that happens while they're in charge, putting them in charge can be an excellent way to make good things happen.

In addition, impatient people can sometimes produce significant progress in a remarkably short period of time; lazy people can figure out how to achieve goals while expending the least effort; and people with stylish clothes and expensive cars often make a positive impression on potential donors, many of whom are also attracted to the outward trappings of success.

For this reason, it's not at all unbelievable that Dean Vader may be the last person in the world whom you'd want as a lifelong friend, but that doesn't necessarily make him ineffective as an academic leader. In fact, some of the very qualities that we find least admirable in him might allow those in his college to achieve success they may not attain under a compassionate, humble, servant leader.

Moreover, our flaws, weaknesses, and imperfections can actually serve as the *source* of benefits for our programs if we direct or channel them in ways that lead to outcomes we desire. Scott Adams, the creator of the cartoon *Dilbert*, notes that he was never able to reach his goal of healthy eating through willpower alone, since willpower is quickly exhausted, although he was readily able to achieve them through sheer laziness, of which he says he has an abundant supply. He simply made sure that the snacks that were easiest to reach and in greatest supply while he worked were foods that were nourishing and wholesome.

> I've learned to use my own laziness in a positive way. I'll always eat what is most convenient during the day, and if the only easy options are healthy, laziness takes me in the best direction. Laziness can be a powerful tool. (Adams, 2014, 193)

As academic leaders, we can do something similar with other aspects of our character that others may regard as less than perfect. We can channel our cowardice into the habit of making sure that our academic programs are always safe and "fly under the radar" when significant budget cuts are made. We can direct our tendencies to be confrontational toward strong advocacy for our colleagues. We can guide our habit of being coldly unemotional toward providing the calm that others rely on in a crisis, and so on. It's merely a matter of finding the best use for our *whole* selves, not just our best selves.

In fact, the line that divides our best features from our flaws is thin and very blurry indeed. The very same attribute that we identify as a virtue in someone we like can be dismissed as a vice in someone we dislike.

What some see as an academic leader's inflexibility, others admire as that person's steadfast consistency and willingness to take a firm position in the style of Martin Luther's declamation to the Reichstag of Worms "Here I stand. I can do nothing else" (*Hier stehe ich. Ich kann nicht anders*). Is an academic leader being greedy, or is that person being ambitious and entrepreneurial? Do we attribute someone's jokes to gentle humor or glib superficiality?

Strong self-confidence can look a lot like arrogance, ingenuity can be interpreted as shrewdness, and a tendency to be inquisitive may be regarded as an inclination to be nosy. What we see in others often depends on what we went looking for: The character of the person does not itself change, but the light in which we view it often does.

SOCIALLY UNPOPULAR OPINIONS

It's also the case that highly effective academic leaders may not always share the perspectives found among many others in their communities or even many others at their institutions.

They don't always support the political candidates that are overwhelmingly popular in the regions where they live. They may not care for children or be comfortable around pets. More specifically, they might be cat lovers in a highly dog-loving community or vice versa. They may be atheists at a faith-based college or fundamentalists at a strongly secular institution. They may, as many people are who grew up in the 1960s or admired that era, be strongly antimilitary at a university with a large

ROTC program or a college that portrays itself as "veteran friendly." Perhaps they work at a school that's a traditional football power but believe that it's wasteful for universities to spend money on nonacademic programs like athletics.

Chances are that, if any of us took an inventory of our beliefs and perspectives on life, everyone would find a number of ways in which he or she was out of the mainstream. We *all* have at least a few opinions that, were we to express them publicly, we'd discover how socially unpopular they were. Being out of sync with a majority of those around us doesn't disqualify us as leaders; it simply makes us human.

Of course, that's not to say that having character flaws and socially unpopular opinions provides us with any surer keys to success than do virtues and broadly supported sentiments. The point is merely that these factors don't necessarily serve as obstacles to success. The important fac-tor—and at this point it should come as no surprise—is whether we are authentic about what we believe, whether we know who we are as indi-viduals and as leaders and act in accordance with our values.

If our hypothetical administrator, Dean Vader, had adopted a differ-ent professional approach and projected the façade of a patient, caring, and generous academic leader, it's highly likely that people would have seen through his pretense before very long, and then his credibility about other matters would also be questioned. Trust can take an incredibly long time to earn, but it can be destroyed in an instant. The very qualities that people may have been willing to tolerate in Dean Vader if he had been candid about them could easily cause a widening rift between him and his faculty if they were hidden and discovered later.

We see examples of this occurrence frequently in society. Someone is elevated as a hero, widely admired, and seen as a paragon of virtue only to be pulled down from their pedestal a short time later when his or her all-too-human flaws are revealed. As James Robilotta says in *Leading Im-perfectly: The Value of Being Authentic for Leaders, Professionals, and Human Beings*:

> We must learn to lead from our faults. As leaders, it is not enough to have messed up and learned from it. While that is the first step, we rarely get to step two: sharing our story. Sharing your story is essential for two reasons: The first is obvious; we want others to learn from our mistakes so they don't make the same ones. . . . The second reason we must lead from our faults is to allow others to see themselves in us. . . .

> We must realize that we were selected for our positions not because we were the most perfect, but because we were the most trusted. (Robilotta, 2015, 37, 39)

People who are perceived by others as perfect are not always the most effective role models. "How can we ever be like them," we wonder, "when we have all these flaws and they have none?" And so, we either stop trying to emulate them or we dismiss them entirely when they're later exposed as not being as entirely perfect as we had thought.

By being themselves—by being comfortable in their own skins and utterly candid about who they are—the Dean Vaders of the world give us permission to be who *we* are. We can feel free to borrow from the successes of these imperfect leaders, understanding that others will similarly be willing to accept our own imperfections, while we simultaneously avoid the qualities that we can't accept in those leaders.

Robilotta notes that some leaders aspire to be heroes while others prefer to be role models. Those who are trying to be heroes seek to conceal their faults and appear perfect, but doing so often causes others to conclude that they could never emulate people who have set standards that (although ultimately illusory) are extremely high. Those who desire to be role models make it clear to others that everyone makes mistakes and that you don't have to be faultless to be effective (Robilotta, 2015, 90–91).

Leading from your flaws frees others to say that they can be like you in ways that they admire while different from you in those aspects of who you are that they can't accept. It also frees them to stop acting like plaster saints and to become authentic academic leaders.

A NEW KIND OF COMPETING VALUES FRAMEWORK

In order for us to become more aware of our position on issues where opposing values may be in competition, it would be useful to have some kind of tool or framework to help assess where our principles and opinions fall relative to those of others.

Unfortunately, the title *Competing Values Framework* has already been taken for a highly popular and valuable way of characterizing the culture of an organization. This framework—sometimes also known as the *Quinn Model*, after its creator Robert E. Quinn—consists of two scales:

1. A vertical axis with the qualities of being *flexible and adaptable* at the top and the qualities of being *stable and controlled* at the bottom.
2. A horizontal axis with an exclusive focus on *internal processes* at the left and an exclusive focus on *external constituents* at the right.

By plotting where an institution falls on these two axes, one can effectively divide organizations into four main cultures:

1. Those that *collaborate* because they are flexible and adaptable with a focus on internal processes.
2. Those that *create* because they are flexible and adaptable with a focus on external constituents.
3. Those that *compete* because they are stable and controlled with a focus on external constituents.
4. Those that *control* because they are stable and controlled with a focus on internal processes. (For more on the Competing Values Framework, see Quinn, 1988; Cameron and Quinn, 2011; and Gmelch and Buller, 2015, 156–59.)

For our purposes, what we need is an inventory that doesn't deal with competing values in organizations but our own tendency to favor one or the other of two competing values. This type of inventory would help us be more authentic in our leadership by alerting us to what our values actually are, even when those values may be out of step with many of those in our community. As an initial attempt toward establishing this sort of alternative competing values inventory, I propose the following exercise:

Read the following sixteen statements and then assign yourself points based on the following scale. If you've not yet been in the situation described, try to imagine how you *would* react if such a situation arose.

- Assign yourself **1 point** if, after reading the statement, you think, "That doesn't describe me at all."
- Assign yourself **2 points** if, after reading the statement, you think, "That describes me a little bit, but not particularly well."
- Assign yourself **3 points** if, after reading the statement, you think, "That describes me sometimes, perhaps as much as half the time."
- Assign yourself **4 points** if, after reading the statement, you think, "That describes me well. I probably feel that way more than half the time."

- Assign yourself **5 points** if, after reading the statement, you think, "That describes me to a T. I feel that way nearly all the time."

At the end of the exercise, you'll be told how to interpret these points. For the moment, simply keep your score for each item separate; don't add the points together.

1. After attending a meeting with the upper administration where I learn information intended for me alone, I tend to share what I learn with others in my program because they have a right to know as much as possible about what's happening at our institution.

2. Given a choice between the certainty of a small bonus now and the possibility of a large bonus several years from now, I'd take the small bonus now. You never know what could happen between now and several years from now.

3. When someone in our program does something wrong that is both serious and intentional, I feel obliged to keep the matter in that person's attention until he or she has made it completely right again, received an appropriate sanction for his or her misdeed, or sincerely apologized for what he or she has done.

4. If only one person in our program could get a raise (and no one would ever find out what I had done), I would take the raise myself rather than assign it to someone else in the program. After all, I work hard—often harder than others who work with me—and I'm less fairly compensated than they are.

5. Colleagues who come to me and share information in confidence can rest assured that I would never tell *anyone* what we discussed in our private meeting, even if it would benefit me to do so.

6. When making investments, I tend to hold those investments for the long term. Changing those investments frequently may create better short-term profits on certain occasions, but I believe that taking the long view is safer and ultimately more profitable.

7. When I have a heated argument with someone, I quickly let those negative feelings go. Maybe the person was just in a bad mood that day (or maybe I was), and a disagreement is not worth losing a friend over. "Forgive and forget," I say.

8. I can honestly say that I take as much pride in the achievements of others in my program as I do in my own achievements. In fact, sometimes I even take more pride in what they do than I do in the recognitions and honors I've received myself.

9. I'm terrible at keeping secrets. If I know something, I'm bound to tell others eventually.

10. Don't count on me to stick to a diet. My best intentions go out the window as soon as I see something I really want to eat that's not on my diet plan.

11. It annoys me when I read in the paper about a thief or murderer getting a light sentence. People should have to pay fully for the wrongs they've done, even if they later regret their actions.

12. I don't find it useful or enjoyable to listen to other people's ideas. My own ideas are usually better than theirs are. Frankly, I think lots of people just talk because they love the sound of their own voices.

13. Sometimes I think I'd make a good spy or secret agent. If I know a secret, you can't get it out of me no matter how much you plead with or threaten me.

14. I'm much better at keeping New Year's resolutions than other people I know. While it's common for others to give up on their good intentions in a week or two, you'll often find me still sticking to my plan in April or May. In fact, many of the changes I resolved to make became permanent aspects of how I live even now.

15. I guess others may think I'm kind of a sucker. If people mistreat me, all they have to do is say, "I'm sorry," and I instantly forgive them. People make mistakes, and I don't see the point of expecting everyone to be perfect or holding a grudge.

16. I'm a strong believer in the concept of servant leadership. To me, leading is about helping others, not benefitting yourself. If I had to make a sacrifice—even a substantial sacrifice—to benefit others in my program or at my institution, I would not hesitate to do so.

Once you have completed this inventory, calculate your scores in the following way. In each case, it is possible for a score to be either a positive or a negative number.

- Add the points you assigned yourself for questions 5 and 13, then subtract from that total your scores for questions 1 and 9. The result is your A Score.

- Add the points you assigned yourself for questions 6 and 14, then subtract from that total your scores for questions 2 and 10. The result is your B Score.

- Add the points you assigned yourself for questions 7 and 15, then subtract from that total your scores for questions 3 and 11. The result is your C Score.
- Add the points you assigned yourself for questions 8 and 16, then subtract from that total your scores for questions 4 and 12. The result is your D Score.

If you haven't guessed it already, the competing values you've been working with throughout this inventory are the Four Dilemmas from the Kidder Paradigm that we considered in chapter 4.

Your A Score reflects your tendency to favor transparency (negative numbers) versus confidentiality (positive numbers). If you calculated your score correctly, it should range from a low of -8 to a high of +8. The lower your score is, the more you tend to choose transparency over confidentiality; the higher your score is, the more likely you are to choose confidentiality over transparency.

Similarly, your B Score reflects your tendency to select short-term benefits over long-term benefits or vice versa. The closer your B Score is to -8, the more attracted you are to short-term gains at the expense of long-term profits. The closer it is to +8, the more you find it useful to "play the long game" rather than reap more immediate rewards.

Your C Score addresses whether you tend to prefer justice or mercy. The closer a score is to -8, the more you tend to favor justice; the closer a score is to +8, the more you tend to favor mercy.

Your D Score deals with the trade-off between yourself and your community. Scores close to -8 indicate a preference for favoring yourself over your community; scores close to +8 indicate the opposite.

Our modified Competing Values Framework indicates just how much overlap there can be between values and matters of opinion or perspectives. Some people are likely to regard a preference of self over others as a vice or at least a character flaw. "It represents selfishness," they might say, "and selfishness is wrong."

Others could argue that a concern for self-preservation is merely common sense. That opinion may not always be socially acceptable, these people might argue, "but it's a valid opinion and happens to represent my personal perspective."

In our effort to achieve as much authenticity as possible by understanding exactly what our values are—even if other people might not support those values or perhaps regard them as character flaws—this modified Competing Values Framework is one more tool we can have in our toolkit for self-understanding. It helps us see how values and opinions guide our actual choices instead of the values we might say we support because "good academic leaders" are expected to support them.

THE POWER OF NEGATIVE THINKING

But being authentic as an academic leader isn't merely about understanding your values and how popular or unpopular your opinions may be. It's also about being aware of your emotions, outlook on life, and personality.

For more than a century, much of the advice provided by American management gurus has focused on the need for leaders to adopt an optimistic and constructive attitude toward their employees. The idea was, in the words of the popular song by Harold Arlen and Johnny Mercer, to "accentuate the positive, eliminate the negative, latch on to the affirmative, and don't mess with Mister In-Between" (Arlen and Mercer, 1944).

Barbara Ehrenreich (2010) has traced a direct line of development from Mary Baker Eddy's Christian Science movement through Norman Vincent Peale's *The Power of Positive Thinking* (1952) and on into Rhonda Byrne's "law of attraction" in *The Secret* (2006). In each case, the argument is that positive attitudes and thoughts will improve one's health, success, or prosperity while negative thoughts will bring about illness, failure, or poverty.

The optimistic, "can do" attitude commonly associated with the American psyche thus became codified as an essential principle of good management: Effective leaders are those who convey confidence even in the face of seemingly impossible odds; ineffective leaders are those who give in to doubt, hesitation, or despair.

Recently, however, a number of authors have begun to question this equation of management success with leadership based in optimism and happiness. In addition to Ehrenreich, authors such as Oettingen (2015), Whippman (2016), Norem (2002), Kashdan and Biswas-Diener (2014), and Held (2001) all argue against the notion that positive attitudes are essential for success; in fact, they suggest that an over-emphasis on happiness and optimism can end up being destructive and lead, not to the desired outcome, but to frustration and disappointment.

But as is so often the case, a reasonable and moderate perspective on this topic is probably closest to the truth. Certainly, optimism and a positive attitude have repeatedly been demonstrated to convey a wide range of benefits.

- In general, optimism conveys greater health benefits than pessimism (Carver, Scheier, and Segerstrom, 2010; Peterson, Seligman, and Vaillant, 1988; and Chang, 2002).
- Optimists are more likely to get hired and promoted than pessimists (Kluemper, Little, and DeGroot, 2009; Kaniel, Massey, and Robinson, 2010).
- Happy, optimistic people tend to be generally more successful across a wide variety of areas than unhappy, pessimistic people (Lyubomirsky, King, and Diener, 2005; Buchanan and Seligman, 1995).
- Optimists are more likely to persevere and ultimately achieve their goals than pessimists (Peterson, 2000; Åstebro, Jeffrey, and Adomdza, 2007).
- Optimists are more resilient and able to cope with setbacks than pessimists (Solberg and Segerstrom, 2006; Dakin, 2015).
- As a result, optimistic undergraduate students are more likely to persist in their studies and graduate on time than are their more pessimistic peers (Solberg, Evans, and Segerstrom, 2009; Chemers, Hu, and Garcia, 2001).

But, despite all these advantages that optimism has, it is also true that negative emotions, including pessimism, have certain advantages as well:

- Pessimists are less likely to drive while fatigued—and thus have traffic accidents—than optimists (Dalziel and Job, 1997).
- Pessimists are more likely to make prudent financial and investment decisions than extreme optimists (Puri and Robinson, 2005).
- While gambling, optimists are more likely than pessimists to engage in risky behaviors like betting more than they can afford and to persist in those behaviors even when they continue to lose (Gibson and Sanbonmatsu, 2004).
- Unlike undergraduates, pessimistic law school students outperform optimistic law school students (Satterfield, Monahan, and Seligman, 1997).

- "Because defensive pessimists do not self-aggrandize as much as strategic optimists, they're more willing to recognize that they make mistakes, and by extension, they may be more open to learning from them" (Norem, 2002, 127).
- Pessimists are more likely to undertake specific actions to solve their problems, while optimists often remain more passive on the assumption that things will get better on their own (Oettingen, 2015, 11–16).
- Optimists tend to be disappointed, at times devastated, when situations don't turn out as well as they had anticipated. Pessimists tend to be more resilient when, as they had predicted, things go poorly, and they are pleasantly surprised when the result turns out to be satisfactory or better (Sweeny and Shepperd, 2010; Cantor and Norem, 1989; Norem, 2002, 42–48).

So, what are we to make of such contradictory results? For one thing, it is overly simplistic to argue that optimism is uniformly a better perspective and explanatory style of events than pessimism. Like so much else, the utility of optimism and pessimism depends on the context.

For this reason, Martin Seligman developed the approach that he called *learned optimism* as a means of tapping into the benefits of optimism when our initial impulse is to be negative. Seligman's basic method may easily be recalled by thinking of the first five letters of the alphabet.

- In Seligman's method, **A stands for Adversity**. What is the problem we're trying to solve? What is the decision we're trying to make?
- **B stands for Belief.** What belief system are we using to interpret that problem or decision? What assumptions are coloring (and perhaps distorting) our view?
- **C stands for Consequences.** What are the results that are likely to follow from that belief system or those assumptions?
- **D stands for Disputation.** Is there another belief system or set of assumptions we could adopt that would cause us to see the situation differently? Could we look at the problem or decision from a different perspective?
- **E stands for Energization**. Would this alternative belief system, set of assumptions, or perspective probably lead us to a better result? If so, wouldn't it be better to approach the problem or decision in that way? (Seligman, 2006, 223–28)

In short, when we feel trapped by our pessimism, it can be helpful to pull back for a second and ask, "What would an optimist do in this situation? And is that approach more likely to bring me to a result I would like than the approach I was considering on my own?"

But, as we've seen, pessimism also at times has its advantages. So, we might want to explore the possibility of a corollary approach that could be called *learned pessimism*. In other words, when we're feeling exuberant about a situation, it can be equally useful to pull back for a second and ask, "What would a *pessimist* do in this situation? And is that approach more likely to bring me to a result I would like than the approach I was considering?"

Learned optimism and learned pessimism can work hand-in-hand and can actually help us make better choices. Consider the following:

- You're thinking of submitting a book proposal to a publisher even though the publisher has turned down five other proposals from you in the past. *What would an optimist do?* Submit the new proposal; maybe this time will be different. *What would a pessimist do?* Avoid the likelihood of yet another rejection. *Which approach could bring about a result that you'd be happier with or less likely to regret?* The optimistic approach, so, in this case, take that alternative.
- You're shopping for a new car and are excited to see a brand new Lamborghini that, although considerably out of your price range, is the most wonderful car you've ever seen. *What would an optimist do?* Buy it; you'll figure out the finances somehow. *What would a pessimist do?* Look for another model more within your price range. *Which approach could bring about a result that you'd be happier with or less likely to regret?* The pessimistic approach, so, in this case, take that alternative.
- You're playing craps in Las Vegas and have already lost nearly $10,000. *What would an optimist do?* Keep playing; you've got to stay in the game to win that money back. *What would a pessimist do?* Walk away from the table; $10,000 is a lot of money, but, if you stay in the game, you're likely to lose far more. *Which approach could bring about a result that you'd be happier with or less likely to regret?* The pessimistic approach, so, in this case, take that alternative.
- You're nervous about admitting that you love someone. *What would an optimist do?* Tell the person; he or she will either say "I love you" back or at least be gratified that you were comfortable enough to

express your feelings. *What would a pessimist do?* Say nothing; what if the other person doesn't feel the same way? *Which approach could bring about a result that you'd be happier with or less likely to regret?* The optimistic approach, so, in this case, take that alternative.

In this way, learned optimism and learned pessimism complement each other by allowing us to see the broader picture and consider alternatives that our initial impulses may have otherwise ignored.

But you may be wondering whether this is really a workable system. After all, it's not impossible that the gambler in our examples may well have made back his or her money by staying at the table or our lover may be mortified by the other person's rejection. It's true that there are times when the system outlined above is not enough to provide the kind of guidance that you need.

In these cases, I find it useful to proceed to a second set of questions. First, could one alternative you're considering, but not the other(s), result in a situation that you absolutely could not live with? If that's the case, then the best strategy is to avoid that alternative. If that's not the case, you get to ask a second question: Which of the alternatives that you're considering could result in the best outcome of all the possible alternatives before you? Take that alternative.

In this way, the gambler will more likely be dissuaded from the risky strategy of staying in the game when his or her losses are substantial. The possibility of losing $100,000 or more is something that he or she probably couldn't live with, even though that outcome may be statistically more probable than recouping the initial loss of $10,000. The bashful lover, on the other hand, has to ask which alternative seems more unbearable: rejection or the regret of not having expressed his or her feelings.

Some people may indeed conclude that rejection would be the worse alternative, and for them remaining silent may indeed be the better choice. But others would conclude that both rejection and regret are unpleasant alternatives and so proceed to the second question. Since the possibility of a favorable response is far preferable to continued uncertainty, they will proceed to express their feelings.

RIGHTEOUS (AND CALCULATED) INDIGNATION

Just as pessimism is sometimes a better option for us than optimism, so can other emotions commonly regarded as negative be better for us than their more positive counterparts. That's the case, at least in certain situations and under specific conditions, for the feeling of anger.

We're often told that anger is a destructive force that we need to avoid. Religious traditions urge us to respond to anger by turning the other cheek (Matthew 5:39) or uttering words of peace (Quran 25:63). We sometimes require people to take courses on anger management but never calm management.

And many of us have experienced how destructive it can be to work for a supervisor who yields frequently to anger; we avoid interactions with that person for fear of becoming a lightning rod for his or her bad temper. Ultimately, people stop telling the supervisor those unwelcome truths that he or she needs to hear, and this lack of awareness leads the supervisor to make additional mistakes and become even angrier.

But anger can also have a positive role. The righteous indignation we feel when confronted by injustice may lead to positive change. Venting our feelings in appropriate ways can purge us of hostility that might eat away at us—sometimes, as in the case of ulcers, literally—if we didn't purge ourselves of our resentment. And Kashdan and Biswas-Diener have documented even more ways in which anger can be beneficial.

- Our anger often motivates us to take action against the things that have provoked us. When those things are genuine annoyances or problems, that action may produce a positive result.
- During negotiations, people who are angry often get a better deal than those who seem complacent.
- A display of anger can eliminate a small threat before it becomes a serious problem. (Kashdan and Biswas-Diener, 2014, 66–79)

In fact, when trying to get our way in the face of opposition, anger can be so effective that we may be tempted to use it strategically, to feign being more irritated by a situation than we actually are. In the short term, this tactic may well prove to be successful. "Oh, I didn't realize it was that important to you," someone might say in response to our outburst and withdraw his or her opposition.

But this type of calculated outrage is rarely effective in the long term. Either you end up being confused with the perennially angry supervisor just mentioned or people begin to recognize that your strategic rancor is merely a ploy and resent being used.

The same thing can be said of other negative emotions. The pain of regret may be bitter, but it prevents us from committing the same mistake again. Yet many of us know someone who repeatedly apologizes for doing something wrong and displays all the outward signs of regret but never alters his or her behavior. After a while, their apologies become meaningless to us.

In the case of shame or embarrassment, we're also likely to be lenient with someone who has done something wrong but seems to be mortified by his or her actions. Nevertheless, if that behavior is repeated and we come to believe that the person's signs of discomfort were feigned, we're likely to be much less forgiving in the future. Even worse, we're likely to lose trust in that person in general, not only with regard for that particular action.

In all these cases there's one common theme: The negative emotion may be unpleasant, but, if those feelings are channeled in the right direction, they can actually lead to positive results. Just as we earlier used our flaws and negative characteristics to lead to a good result, we can also do much the same thing with our negative emotions.

Sadness, regret, and shame tend to bring a group closer together. For example, when someone is demonstrably sad, even those who are indifferent or hostile to that person will usually set aside those feelings and rally around them. (For a study that demonstrates this process in action, see Dijk, De Jong, and Peters, 2009.)

It's only when people try to manipulate others by *pretending* to experience a negative emotion that significant damage is done. Although the false emotions may initially be accepted as genuine, the fact that the person's behavior doesn't change eventually indicates to others that they were being used.

As we've seen repeatedly, it's authenticity that becomes the key expectation. Those who work with us will understand if every now and then we're angry, remorseful, or ashamed. What they won't understand is our abuse of their sympathies by adopting the false flag of feigned emotions.

THE JOYS OF SADNESS

Even the kingpin of all negative emotions—sadness—is not without its positive aspects. If that weren't the case, the Greeks would never have invented tragedy, movies in which the protagonist dies would never succeed at the box office, and country music would have no market. There are simply times when we actually *enjoy* being sad.

Please note that I'm making a distinction between occasional, voluntary sadness and chronic, crippling sadness such as occurs with clinical depression. The types of sadness I have in mind always retain some element of consent; we willingly accept these experiences, and, when they cease to be pleasant or useful, we reject them.

Moreover, sadness can be *useful*. "Expressions of sadness communicate to others that you are in trouble and need help; expressions of happiness signal to others that everything is fine" (Kashdan and Biswas-Diener, 2014, 113). Kashdan and Biswas-Diener also cite studies indicating that happy people can be too trusting and that those who are sad often make more accurate assessments of another person's intentions (Kashdan and Biswas-Diener, 2014, 102–4).

Joseph Forgas has gone even further and demonstrated that sadness can be beneficial for cognition and can help with issues such as memory, motivation, and making appropriate social judgments (Forgas, 2017). The sadness of re-experiencing painful moments as part of therapy can, with proper guidance and under the right conditions, lead to breakthroughs and overall improvement of mental health.

Moreover, excessive happiness is sometimes interpreted (at least within certain cultures) as an indication of shallowness or even a lack of intelligence; the "brooding intellectual" and "glowering Russian poet" may be stereotypes, but they are stereotypes that clearly affect the way in which very happy and very sad people may be perceived by others.

The point is not that unhappy people make better leaders than happy people any more than it is that happy people necessarily make better leaders than unhappy people. Rather sadness resembles other negative emotions in that it can lead to positive results if its energy is channeled in the right direction. That's a phenomenon familiar to anyone who returned to work shortly after the loss of a loved one.

Being back in a routine and doing productive work can be comforting, and many people also find themselves unexpectedly tapping into new sources of creativity and efficiency. In fact, it's not at all uncommon to look back on those experiences and be surprised by the sheer amount of highly productive work one accomplished during a period that appeared to be filled with so much grief.

As Julie Norem observes in her delightfully named book *The Positive Power of Negative Thinking* (2002):

> Research on creativity and mood confirms the stylistic differences [between happy and unhappy people]. Positive mood increases creativity, *if* by creativity we mean the number of ideas people generate (or how quickly they generate them); negative mood increases creativity *if* by creativity we mean the number of workable, high quality ideas. (Norem, 2002, 147)

In short, when it comes to creativity and productivity, both happy people and sad people have certain advantages over one another. As Kashdan and Biswas-Diener conclude, "[Q]uit labeling your inner states as good or bad or positive or negative, and start thinking of them as useful or not useful for any given situation" (Kashdan and Biswas-Diener, 2014, 202).

FORCEFUL VERSUS REFLECTIVE LEADERSHIP

Unfortunately, you don't find these ideas being discussed at many leadership conferences or in most management books. The speakers at those conferences and the authors of those books tend to have backgrounds in the military, athletics, or sales, and their message (not infrequently combined with a tacit or explicit evangelistic message) is, "Get excited. Get motivated. Get loud. And get going."

You can detect the consistency of this theme from the titles alone:

- Pat Williams's *Extreme Winning: 12 Keys to Unlocking the Winner Within You* (Williams and Kerasotis, 2015), *The Success Intersection: What Happens When Your Talent Meets Your Passion* (Williams and Denney, 2017), and *Coaching Your Kids to Be Leaders: The Keys to Unlocking Their Potential* (Williams, Denney, and Wooden, 2014);
- Donald Trump's *Think Big and Kick Ass: In Business and in Life* (2007), *Time to Get Tough: Making America #1 Again* (Trump, 2011), and *Think Like a Champion: An Informal Education in Business and Life* (Trump and McIver, 2010);

- Brian Tracy's *No Excuses!: The Power of Self-Discipline* (2010), *Just Shut Up and Do It: 7 Steps to Conquer Your Goals* (2016), and *Maximum Achievement: The Proven System of Strategies and Skills That Will Unlock Your Hidden Powers to Succeed* (1993).

Perhaps two works by Grant Cardone best sum up this genre: *Be Obsessed or Be Average* (2016) and *If You're Not First, You're Last* (2010).

A similar spirit permeates Amway conventions, Tony Robbins's Unleash the Power Within events, and religious services of the Rick Warren (*The Purpose-Driven Life*, 2002) and Joel Osteen (*Your Best Life Now*, 2004) variety. They generate the energy (and at times the noise) of high school pep rallies and are designed to leave the participants excited, energized, and ready to win.

The conclusion one draws is that, if you want to be a leader, you have to be dynamic, energetic, and inspired. Effective leaders are "in your face," demand 110 percent of your commitment, and never settle for anything less than the best. Those who aren't tough aren't worthy to lead. In fact, they're nothing more than losers.

Nevertheless, in a refreshing response to this school of thought about leadership, Susan Cain offers us an alternative in her book *Quiet: The Power of Introverts in a World That Can't Stop Talking* (2013). Cain's point isn't merely that introverts and extroverts have different ways of responding to social situations, but also that there's a valid style of leadership common to introverts, a style that is often far more effective than the bold, brash, "I'm not here to make friends" style of extroverts.

Confident, extroverted leaders more quickly gain people's trust, but reflective, introverted leaders frequently make better decisions. Cain points to phenomena like the *winner's curse* in which a competition among bidders becomes a battle of egos rather than an accurate assessment of whatever it is they're bidding for is worth. Someone who is highly confident and extroverted is likely to keep raising his or her bid "as a matter of principle," merely to come out victorious, even if it means paying far more than the prize is worth.

A more introverted and reflective bidder tends to drop out of the competition when price begins to exceed value (yet another case in which the vice of being a quitter may be more useful than the virtue of being determined) (Cain, 2013, 50–52).

In addition, Cain cites a study conducted by Adam Grant, Francesca Gino, and David Hofmann demonstrating that, although extroverted leaders tend to have better results when dealing with passive employees or followers, introverted leaders tend to have better results when dealing with proactive employees or followers (Grant, Gino, and Hofmann, 2011; Cain, 2013, 55–58).

In the organizational culture of higher education, where many people tend to be highly proactive—think, for example, of highly engaged faculty members and highly motivated development officers—an introverted style of leadership can thus bring with it many advantages.

That factor may help explain why there often seems to be a disconnect at leadership conferences in higher education between the messages conveyed by keynote speakers, many of whom are invited because of their success as leaders in corporate or athletic environments, and the reaction of the audience. "Well, that was interesting," people often say on leaving these sessions, "but it just didn't relate to who I am or what I do."

In illustrating why introverts can be just as effective as extroverts (and often more so) when working as leaders in higher education, we seem to have wandered very far from our initial subject in this chapter. And we have.

After all, being an introvert shouldn't be equated with being lazy, compulsive, greedy, unpredictable, or narcissistic. The personality you have isn't as controllable as the behavior you engage in. And we may believe that, although many people would classify laziness, greed, and the like as serious faults, no one is likely to feel the same way about being reflective or reserved. But Cain argues otherwise:

> Introversion—along with its cousins sensitivity, seriousness, and shyness—is now a second-class personality trait, somewhere between a disappointment and a pathology. Introverts living under the Extrovert Ideal are . . . discounted because of a trait that goes to the core of who they are. Extroversion is an enormously appealing personality style, but we've turned it into an oppressive standard to which most of us feel we must conform. (Cain, 2013, 4)

But authentic academic leadership involves recognition, acknowledgment, and acceptance of *all* the dimensions of who you are, not merely the socially popular dimensions or the traits—vision! authority! confidence!—that certain management books say all "great" leaders possess or, if we were to take a contrarian point of view, socially unacceptable opinions or vices.

Leadership is simply too complex a phenomenon to be reducible to a recipe of ingredients, no matter how long or well-intentioned that list may be. You simply don't have to be a perfect person—or even someone else's idea of a perfect leader—in order to lead effectively.

Regardless of whatever values you have, whatever personality you possess, and whatever limitations you may see in yourself, it's possible for you to be an effective leader. You just have to understand who you are, own that identity, and then use those values, personality traits, and perceived limitations to bring about results that are beneficial to your institution and program.

THE LEADERSHIP APPROACH INVENTORY

The modified competing values exercise that we conducted earlier in this chapter provided us with one more tool for understanding how our values and opinions affect our decisions and other behavior. But it would also be useful to have some way of helping us see the larger picture.

How, in other words, do values, personality (specifically our tendency toward introversion or extraversion), and positive versus negative emotions all fit together? To what extent do we conform to or deviate from most people's stereotype of what a "typical academic leader" should be? As must be clear by now, there really is no such thing as a *typical* academic leader. Each of us is unique in our own ways.

But that doesn't stop the people we work with—and perhaps more importantly the people who interview and select us for leadership roles—from having some mental model of what an effective leader should be like. And, if we're going to be authentic in the way we work with others, it would be helpful to know how close we are to that mental model. That doesn't mean that we're going to change what we do and how we act; it merely means that we'll have a better understanding of how our deeds and actions are perceived or misinterpreted by others.

The short assessment that I use to gain this insight is the Leadership Approach Inventory. It works in many ways like the competing values exercise that we did earlier in this chapter. In fact, it's a good idea to complete that exercise shortly before taking this inventory so that you've recently reflected on what your values are and the degree to which those values are similar to or different from other academic leaders you know.

As with the other exercise, this inventory consists of reading each of the fifteen statements in the inventory and then doing the following:

- Assign yourself **1 point** if, after reading the statement, you think, "That doesn't describe me at all."
- Assign yourself **2 points** if, after reading the statement, you think, "That describes me a little bit, but not particularly well."
- Assign yourself **3 points** if, after reading the statement, you think, "That describes me sometimes, perhaps as much as half the time."
- Assign yourself **4 points** if, after reading the statement, you think, "That describes me well. I probably feel that way more than half the time."
- Assign yourself **5 points** if, after reading the statement, you think, "That describes me to a T. I feel that way nearly all the time."

Once again, you'll be told how to interpret these points at the end of the exercise. For the time being, simply keep your score for each item separate; don't add the points together.

1. Many of my core values or beliefs strike me as out of the mainstream when I compare them to those of most other academic leaders.
2. I find it challenging to make small talk with people, particularly with those I don't know.
3. Compared to other people in higher education, I'm probably less prone to see the humor in many situations that arise.
4. I often feel the need to conceal how I really feel about certain matters because, if I said what I really believed, others would not approve.
5. I often try to get out of purely social gatherings or, if I feel I have to go, I either leave early or stay but feel uncomfortable.
6. The incompetence of others makes me angry and, when that happens, I express my anger openly and (in many cases) loudly.
7. If those I work with knew my real views on many issues, they'd probably lose respect for me or not like me as much as they do.
8. When I have nothing to do, I don't feel productive; I feel irritated or frustrated and believe that I'm wasting my time.
9. I probably feel more guilt or regret about my past actions and decisions than most academic leaders feel about theirs.

10. I sometimes feel that I need to act on the basis of how people expect "a good academic leader" to act rather than how I really feel about the issue.

11. I prefer giving a presentation to hundreds of people than mingling with them afterward or chatting casually with only a few people I don't know well.

12. I'm really more of a "glass half empty" than "glass half full" type of person, particularly with regards to my professional responsibilities.

13. I don't believe that academic leaders are necessarily most effective when they act in the ways that most people traditionally regard as "good" or "virtuous."

14. I prefer to text or e-mail rather than to communicate on the phone. In fact, I often screen calls, even from people I know well.

15. Things that tend not to bother other people often make me anxious. In fact, I frequently feel anxious even though I can't pinpoint the cause.

Once you have assigned yourself a score of 1 to 5 for each of these statements, transfer your scores to the grid in figure 5.1.

A	B	C
1.	2.	3.
4.	5.	6.
7.	8.	9.
10.	11.	12.
13.	14.	15.
_____ Total for Column A	_____ Total for Column B	_____ Total for Column C

Figure 5.1.

When you total each column, the result should range from a low of 5 to a high of 25. Those total scores can then be plotted by placing dots or Xs on the three axes of figure 5.2.

As you can see from the labels on those axes, your A Score relates to how well you believe your values conform to those of most academic leaders. Your B Score relates to your tendency toward extraversion or introversion. And your C Score reflects where you fall on a number of emotional scales (Question #3: humor versus seriousness, Question #6: anger versus composure, Question #9: guilt or regret versus self-acceptance, Question #12: optimism versus pessimism, and Question #15: anxiety versus calm).

The questions are structured in such a way that lower scores are associated with the approaches and personality traits of what most people *expect* in a "typical" academic leader: mainstream values, extraversion, optimism, self-confidence, joy, and the like. For this reason, if you connect the three dots or Xs you plotted on figure 5.2, the size and shape of the resulting triangle provide you with a clear, graphic illustration of the extent to which you see yourself conforming to the "expected norm" for academic leaders.

For instance, the example depicted in figure 5.3 is a fairly small, tight triangle (A Score = 7, B Score = 7, C Score = 5). If your diagram is similar, you see yourself as adhering rather closely to the values, personality type, and emotional response of what many people would regard as a "stereotypical academic leader."

The example depicted in figure 5.4 is quite different. The triangle is large and open (A Score = 22, B Score = 18, C Score = 20), indicating that this person sees himself or herself as deviating quite broadly from the "stereotypical academic leader."

In figure 5.5, we find a diagram that is quite literally "eccentric," or "off-center": The person deviates far from traditional expectations in the areas of personality and emotion (B Score = 20, C Score = 22), but believes that he or she conforms to the mainstream in the area of socially admired values (A Score = 6).

The advantage of the Leadership Approach Inventory, therefore, is that it gives you a very quick and easily understood insight into how you view yourself relative to what others may initially expect from an academic leader.

- If your triangle is small and clings to the center of the diagram, you view yourself as conventional.
- If your triangle is large but still largely centered on the diagram, you view yourself as atypical.
- And if your triangle skews to any side of the diagram, you view yourself as eccentric: like most leaders in certain ways, but highly distinctive in others.

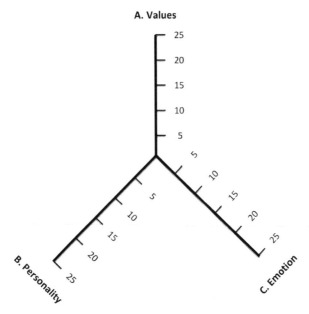

Figure 5.2. Scale for the Leadership Approach Inventory

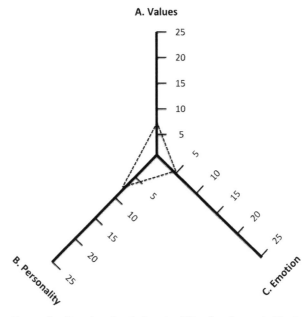

Figure 5.3. Example of an Academic Leader Who Conforms to Typical Expectations

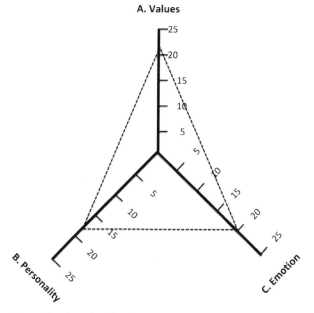

Figure 5.4.   Example of an Academic Leader Who Deviates Sharply from Typical Expectations

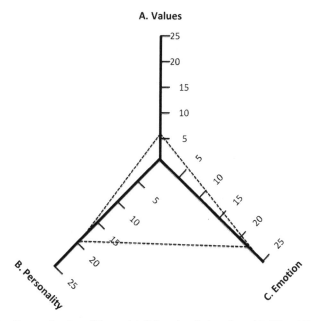

Figure 5.5.   Example of an "Eccentric" Academic Leader with Mixed Results

What, then, can you do with that insight? In order to answer this question, we'll need to pull together the results of all the inventories and exercises in this book, an activity that we'll conduct in the next and final chapter.

KEY POINTS FROM CHAPTER 5

- Most discussions of authentic academic leadership are inconsistent in that they first suggest that leaders should be true to their own values, but then attempt to dictate what those values should be.
- Our flaws, shortcomings, and socially unpopular opinions can become beneficial to our academic programs if we recognize them for what they are and channel them toward constructive goals.
- In a similar way, it is not effective to expect all academic leaders to be optimistic, extroverted, happy, and free from anger. Those traits and tendencies, too, can be beneficial to an academic program if approached correctly.
- The modified competing values exercise and the Leadership Approach Inventory are useful tools that academic leaders can use to better understand their values and the degree to which they see their values, personality, and emotions as conforming to or deviating from the "norm" most people associate with the "typical academic leader."

REFERENCES

Adams, S. (2014). *How to fail at almost everything and still win big: Kind of the story of my life*. New York: Portfolio/Penguin.

Arlen, H. (music), & Mercer, J. (lyrics). (1944). *Ac-Cent-Tchu-Ate the Positive* [Song.] Recorded by Johnny Mercer, the Pied Pipers, and the Paul Weston Orchestra, Capitol Records.

Åstebro, T., Jeffrey, S. A., & Adomdza, G. K. (July 2007). Inventor perseverance after being told to quit: The role of cognitive biases. *Journal of Behavioral Decision Making. 20*(3), 253–72.

Buchanan, G. M. C., & Seligman, M. E. P. (1995). *Explanatory style*. Hillsdale, NJ: L. Erlbaum.

Byrne, R. (2006). *The secret*. New York: Atria.

Cain, S. (2013). *Quiet: The power of introverts in a world that can't stop talking*. New York: Broadway.

Cameron, K. S., & Quinn, R. E. (2011). *Diagnosing and changing organizational culture: Based on the competing values framework*. (3rd. Ed.) San Francisco: Jossey-Bass.

Cantor, N., & Norem, J. K. (1989). Defensive pessimism and stress and coping. *Social Cognition. 7*(2), 92–112.

Cardone, G. (2010). *If you're not first, you're last: Sales strategies to dominate your market and beat your competition.* Hoboken, NJ: Wiley.

Cardone, G. (2016). *Be obsessed or be average.* New York: Portfolio/Penguin.

Carver, C. S., Scheier, M. F., & Segerstrom, S. C. (2010). Optimism. *Clinical Psychology Review. 30*(7), 879–89.

Chang, E. C. (2002). *Optimism & pessimism: Implications for theory, research, and practice.* Washington, DC: American Psychological Association.

Chemers, M. M., Hu, L., & Garcia, B. F. (2001). Academic self-efficacy and first-year college student performance and adjustment. *Journal of Educational Psychology. 93,* 55–64.

Dakin, J. (2015). When the going gets tough. . . . In Dakin, J. (2015). *Learn to dance on a moving carpet: How to create a balanced and meaningful life.* Samford Valley, QLD: Australian Academic Press: 69–79.

Dalziel, J. R., & Job, R. F. (1997). Motor vehicle accidents, fatigue and optimism bias in taxi drivers. *Accident Analysis and Prevention. 29*(4), 489–94.

Dijk, C., De Jong, P., & Peters, M. L. (2009). The remedial value of blushing in the context of transgressions and mishaps. *Emotion. 9*(2), 287–91.

Ehrenreich, B. (2010). *Bright-sided: How positive thinking is undermining America.* New York: Picador.

Forgas, J. P. (February 2017). Can sadness be good for you?: On the cognitive, motivational, and interpersonal benefits of mild negative affect. *Australian Psychologist. 52*(1), 3–13.

George, B. (2003). *Authentic leadership: Rediscovering the secrets to creating lasting value.* San Francisco: Jossey-Bass.

Gibson, B., & Sanbonmatsu, D. M. (February, 2004). Optimism, pessimism, and gambling: The downside of optimism. *Personality and Social Psychology Bulletin. 30*(2), 149–60.

Gmelch, W. H., & Buller, J. L. (2015). *Building academic leadership capacity: A guide to best practices.* San Francisco: Jossey-Bass.

Grant, A. M., Gino, F., & Hofmann, D. A. (2011). Reversing the extraverted leadership advantage: The role of employee proactivity. *Academy of Management Journal. 54*(3), 528–50.

Heinlein, R. A. (1988). *Time enough for love: The lives of Lazarus Long.* New York: Ace Books.

Held, B. S. (2001). *Stop smiling, start kvetching: A 5-step guide to creative complaining.* New York: St. Martin's Griffin.

Kaniel, R., Massey, C., & Robinson, D. T. (2010). *The importance of being an optimist: Evidence from labor markets.* Cambridge, MA: National Bureau of Economic Research.

Kashdan, T., & Biswas-Diener, R. (2014). *The upside of your dark side: Why being your whole self—not just your "good" self—drives success and fulfillment.* New York: Hudson Street.

Kluemper, D. H., Little, L. M., & DeGroot, T. (February 2009). State or trait: Effects of state optimism on job-related outcomes. *Journal of Organizational Behavior. 30*(2), 209–31.

LeRoy, M. (producer), & Fleming, V. (director). (1939). *The Wizard of Oz.* [Motion Picture]. USA: Metro Goldwyn Mayer.

Lyubomirsky, S., King, L., & Diener, E. (2005). The benefits of frequent positive affect: Does happiness lead to success? *Psychological Bulletin. 131*(6), 803–55.

Norem, J. K. (2002.) *The positive power of negative thinking: Using defensive pessimism to manage anxiety and perform at your peak.* New York: Basic Books.

Oettingen, G. (2015). *Rethinking positive thinking: Inside the new science of motivation.* New York: Current.

Osteen, J. (2004). *Your best life now: 7 steps to living at your full potential.* New York: Warner Books.

Peale, N. V. (1952). *The power of positive thinking.* New York: Prentice-Hall.

Peterson, C. (2000). The future of optimism. *American Psychologist. 55*, 44–55.

Peterson, C., Seligman, M. E., & Vaillant, G. E. (July 1988). Pessimistic explanatory style is a risk factor for physical illness: A thirty-five-year longitudinal study. *Journal of Personality and Social Psychology. 55*(1), 23–27.

Pressman, E. R. (producer), & Stone, O. (director). (1987). *Wall Street* [Motion Picture]. USA: Twentieth Century Fox.

Puri, M., & Robinson, D. T. (2005). *Optimism and economic choice.* Cambridge, MA: National Bureau of Economic Research.

Quinn, R. E. (1988). *Beyond rational management: Mastering the paradoxes and competing demands of high performance.* San Francisco: Jossey-Bass.

Robilotta, J. T. (2015). *Leading imperfectly: The value of being authentic for leaders, professionals, and human beings.* Lake Placid, NY: Aviva.

Satterfield, J. M., Monahan, J., & Seligman, M. E. (1997). Law school performance predicted by explanatory style. *Behavioral Sciences & the Law. 15*(1), 95–105.

Seligman, M. E. P. (2006). *Learned optimism: How to change your mind and your life.* New York: Vintage.

Solberg, N. L., Evans, D. R., & Segerstrom, S. C. (August, 2009). Optimism and college retention: Mediation by motivation, performance, and adjustment. *Journal of Applied Social Psychology. 39*(8), 1887–912.

Solberg, N. L., & Segerstrom, S. C. (2006). Dispositional optimism and coping: A meta-analytic review. *Personality and Social Psychology Review. 10*, 235–51.

Sweeny, K., & Shepperd, J. A. (October, 2010). The costs of optimism and the benefits of pessimism. *Emotion. 10*(5), 750–53.

Terry, R. W., & Cleveland, H. (1993). *Authentic leadership: Courage in action.* San Francisco: Jossey-Bass Publishers.

Tracy, B. (1993). *Maximum achievement: The proven system of strategies and skills that will unlock your hidden powers to succeed.* New York: Simon & Schuster.

Tracy, B. (2010). *No excuses!: The power of self-discipline.* New York: Vanguard Press.

Tracy, B. (2016). *Just shut up and do it!: 7 steps to conquer your goals.* Naperville, IL: Simple Truths/Sourcebooks.

Trump, D. (2007). *Think big and kick ass: In business and in life.* New York: HarperCollins.

Trump, D. (2011). *Time to get tough: Making America #1 again.* Washington, DC: Regnery.

Trump, D., & McIver, M. (2010). *Think like a champion: An informal education in business and life.* New York: Vanguard Press.

Ulrich, L. T. (1976). Vertuous women found: New England ministerial literature, 1668–1735. *American Quarterly. 28*(1), 20–40.

Walumbwa, F. O., Peterson, S. J., Avolio, B. J., Wernsing, T. S., & Gardner, W. L. (February, 2008). Authentic leadership: Development and validation of a theory-based measure. *Journal of Management.* 34(1), 89–126.

Warren, R. (2002). *The purpose-driven life.* Grand Rapids, MI: Zondervan.

Whippman, R. (2016). *America the anxious: How our pursuit of happiness is creating a nation of nervous wrecks.* New York: St. Martin's Press.

Williams, P., & Denney, J. (2017). *The success intersection: What happens when your talent meets your passion.* Grand Rapids, MI: Revell.

Williams, P., Denney, J., & Wooden, J. (2014). *Coaching your kids to be leaders: The keys to unlocking their potential.* New York: FaithWords.

Williams, P., & Kerasotis, P. (2015). *Extreme winning: 12 keys to unlocking the winner within you.* Deerfield Beach, FL: Health Communications.

RESOURCES

Berns, G. (2010). *Iconoclast: A neuroscientist reveals how to think differently.* Boston: Harvard Business Press.

Butterfield, S. (1985). *Amway, the cult of free enterprise.* Boston: South End Press.

Hackenbracht, J., & Tamir, M. (September 12, 2010). Preferences for sadness when eliciting help: Instrumental motives in sadness regulation. *Motivation and Emotion.* 34(3), 306–15.

Lennick, D., & Kiel, F. (2011). *Moral intelligence 2.0: Enhancing business performance and leadership success in turbulent times.* Upper Saddle River, NJ: Prentice Hall.

Parrott, W. G. (ed.). (2014). *The positive side of negative emotions.* New York: Guilford.

Robbins, K., & Cooper, C. (2014). *What makes you tick.* St. Louis, MO: Archer's Press.

SIX

Charting a Course Based on Values

Sometimes, in order to follow our moral compass . . . , we have to make unpopular decisions or stand up for what we believe in. It can be difficult and even frightening to go against the grain, whether it's a personal disagreement with a friend, partner, or family member or a professional decision that affects coworkers and colleagues. . . . We have to stand up for what we believe in, even when we might not be popular for it. Honesty starts with being ourselves, authentic and true to who we are and what we believe in, and that may not always be popular, but it will always let you follow your dreams and your heart.
—Tabatha Coffey, 2012

Throughout our exploration of authentic academic leadership, we've identified the values that we believe are most important to us; clarified those values by reducing what was initially a long list of principles we believe in to a much shorter list of principles that define who we are as human beings; refined those values by testing with such techniques as the Krathwohl Affective Domain Taxonomy, the Johari Window, and A/B Dilemmas; and come to recognize that even if others regard our values as character flaws or dismiss them as socially unacceptable, our values can be directed in such a way that our programs and institutions benefit as a result. At this point, it's now possible for each of us to chart a course for our academic leadership based on our own authentic values.

REVISITING THE CONCEPTS OF PRODUCT, PROCESS, AND PRINCIPLE

In chapter 2, we distinguished among three different kinds of motivation:

- Product-oriented motivation occurs when a leader is attracted by the desire to achieve a specific goal.
- Process-oriented motivation occurs when a leader's focus is directed more toward the activity that will produce a goal than the goal itself.
- Principle-oriented motivation occurs when a leader's values inspire the leader to act in a certain way regardless of product (goal) or process (the system in which he or she operates).

Both from the way in which chapter 2 is structured and this book's emphasis on the importance of values, it's a logical conclusion that I believe product-oriented and process-oriented motivations are bad, while principle-oriented motivations are good. The fact of the matter is that I do believe that's true, but only as a *general corrective* to the general direction that higher education is taking today.

Strategic planning and performance-based budgeting systems generally cause institutions and programs to over-emphasize products and goals, while accreditation bodies and assessment strategies generally cause institutions and programs to over-emphasize processes and procedures.

Certainly having the goal of making sure that students succeed in their academic programs and graduate on time isn't an unworthy objective, but, when graduation rates cause an obsession for an institution and sideline all emphasis on whether the students are actually growing intellectually as scholars, citizens, and individuals, something has gone wrong.

Similarly, periodically making a case to peer institutions that our standards are rigorous and that we're following our stated procedures isn't a useless activity; however, an institution's priorities seem misaligned when scarce resources have to be directed away from teaching and research to hire staff members to prepare accreditation reports.

By encouraging academic leaders to renew their emphasis on principles, we can help rebalance the decision-making processes of institutions so that product and process are neither ignored nor exaggerated. One useful way of restoring this balance is to think in terms of what the cartoonist Scott Adams calls systems, not goals (Adams, 2014, 30–34). We encountered one of his systems in the last chapter: Adams's reliance on laziness instead of willpower to eat in a healthy manner. But his principle has a broader application.

We might make the distinction between what Adams calls systems and goals in the following manner. Goals include objectives like "I want to lose forty pounds," "I want to retire before I'm sixty," and, in the realm of academic leadership, "Our institution will be included among the Top 10 National Universities in the *U.S. News & World Report* national ranking."

The problem with goals is that we tend to grade them pass or fail. Losing thirty-five pounds might be a wonderful thing. Retiring when you're sixty-two might give you lots of flexibility to do the things you like. And becoming one of the top fifty schools in the *U.S. News & World Report* national ranking might be a phenomenal achievement, but you'd still feel like a failure because you didn't meet your goal.

Even worse, your sense of accomplishment even if you *did* achieve your goals is likely to be short-lived because reaching one goal usually just causes us to set the next goal. Now that you lost forty pounds, you'll want to exercise until you lose another five pounds. (Out of such practices, eating disorders develop.) Now that you retired at age fifty-eight, you'll want to start that novel you always said you'd write—and then feel like a failure if you don't finish it or can't get it published. Now that you reached your goal of being in the Top 10 National Universities in the *U.S. News & World Report* national ranking, you'll drive the faculty and staff nuts until you crack the top five (and probably never make it because dozens of other universities are also trying to claw their way into the top five).

In other words, although we think of goals as being great motivators, they prove to bring disappointments. If, for whatever reason, we cannot reach the targets we set as our goals, we feel like failures. And if we do reach our goals, we keep setting new goals until we *become* failures.

If Lawrence Peter's eponymous Peter Principle (Peter and Hull, 1969) was that people tend to rise in an organization until they reach their level of incompetence, this new principle might be that people succeed at goal setting until they reach their level of failure. It's a no-win proposition.

That's why Adams says that systems are better than goals. A system might be something like eating in a healthy manner, exercising regularly, and seeking out employment that you find both interesting and challenging. In the realm of academic leadership, a system might be something like Valencia College's "Big Idea" that "Anyone Can Learn Anything Under the Right Conditions" (Trustee Education & Preparation, 2017) or North Carolina State University's commitment to redesigning learning spaces from the ground up to incorporate the latest discoveries about how people learn best (Adaptive Learning Spaces and Interactive Content Environments, n.d.).

A goal is a target that you hit or (more often) miss. A system is a strategy that carries you forward in a continual path of improvement. If you set yourself the goal of becoming a college president, but your career plateaus when you become a dean, your tendency will be to be disappointed over "what might have been." But if you adopt the system of always seeking interesting and challenging jobs, mastering them, and then moving on to new opportunities, your system will carry you to a continual series of successes.

Goals, in other words, anticipate *one* future, a future that may or may not materialize. Systems prepare you for many possible futures. And that's an important distinction. A lot of what happens to us either as individuals or as members of our institutions is beyond our personal control. In order to be hired as a dean or provost at our "dream institution," we're dependent on others being willing to select us.

And sometimes what happens is just a matter of luck. A job opens up because someone dies (bad luck for them, but a potential opportunity for us). A donor happens to appear on the scene at just the right moment to fund the project that will make our reputation. We work on a research project for years while meeting with only a moderate level of interest and then suddenly, for a reason we had absolutely nothing to do with, our research area becomes a hot topic that everyone's talking about.

You can't plan for these eventualities, and that's where the weaknesses in goal setting and planning come in. A system helps you *prepare*, not just plan. And when you're prepared, you'll be ready to take full advantage of circumstances when luck comes your way.

In addition, systems don't require willpower to keep them going in the way that goals do. In a famous study by Roy Baumeister of Florida State University, participants that were tempted by a delicious and fragrant plate of warm cookies gave up on a puzzle much faster than those who were "tempted" by a plate of radishes (Baumeister, 1998). Members of the first group had simply exhausted their willpower in trying to resist the urge to eat the cookies and didn't have the mental or emotional stamina to persist with the puzzle.

As academic leaders, we see a similar phenomenon with our institutions' strategic planning efforts. Strategic planning usually relies on goals, targets, and metrics. At the beginning of the process, there's often a great deal of willpower directed toward achieving those objectives.

But, as Baumeister demonstrated, willpower is a limited resource: When faculty members exhaust their limited supply on the other requirements we impose on them—such as excellence in teaching, research, and service, the activities for which they are rewarded in our evaluation systems—they lose their enthusiasm for pursuing strategic goals.

That's why, despite every president or chancellor's promise that "This is going to be one strategic plan that doesn't just sit on the shelf," most strategic plans end up doing exactly that after the first year or two.

But while Adams's concept of "systems, not goals" is useful, I'd go one step further and add an emphasis on values into the mix. Values help you decide which systems are right for you and steer you clear of those systems that are wrong for you.

Leaving your job for a better paying alternative may be a system—it may even be a fairly effective system—but that may not be your best choice in systems if you feel you have to sacrifice your lifelong devotion to serving the underprivileged just to end up lonely and regretful in a corner office somewhere. Similarly, always buying the least expensive option may be a system, but it's not a particularly good system if the low quality of what you buy ends up costing you more in the long run because of repairs and replacements.

Probably the most effective strategy academic leaders can adopt is one that takes into account all three of these concerns: goals, systems, and values. Or, to return to the terminology I introduced in chapter 2, the strategy would reintegrate our Product-, Process-, and Principle-Oriented Motivations.

We can think of how this strategy would operate in the following way. If, as we saw, a Product-Oriented Motivation was at the heart of Robert House's influential Path-Goal Theory, then what authentic academic leaders might want to pursue is something more similar to a **Values-Path-Goal Theory**.

Leaders' values determine the paths they will take and incorporate such elements as leadership style, strategic direction, and personal philosophy. Those paths, to return to Adams's expression, are the academic leaders' *systems*. These systems will then enable academic leaders to reach certain goals.

But those goals may look somewhat different from those found in a traditional strategic plan that emphasizes precise metrics and key performance indicators. In order to avoid the temptation to cut corners, game the system, or use the ends to justify the means, goals should be set as general aspirations rather than as specific make-or-break objectives.

An example will help clarify how this strategy works in the real world. Georgian Court University (GCU) in Lakewood, New Jersey, was founded in 1908 and provides a comprehensive liberal arts education in the Roman Catholic tradition. As part of its 2018–2019 reaffirmation of accreditation by the Middle States Commission on Higher Education, it decided to create a *strategic compass* (Buller, 2015, 122–27) as an alternative to a more traditional and restrictive strategic plan.

With a strategic compass, instead of trying to envision what the world of higher education will be like ten, fifteen, or twenty years in the future and establish specific metrics based on those assumptions (which are likely to prove wrong in any case), a school sets itself on course in a general direction, guided by its values and understanding of its distinctive role as an institution, with a more detailed tactical plan for perhaps the next three to five years.

In the case of GCU, the process is rooted in its commitment to Mercy Core Values, the principles that are at the heart of the Sisters of Mercy tradition that continues to shape the school's vision: respect, integrity, justice, compassion, and service (Mission and Mercy Core Values, n.d.).

GCU's strategic compass then became the path or system by which those values would carry the institution into the future. There are several advantages of this approach over the way in which most other colleges and universities conduct strategic planning.

First, by only setting specific target goals and dates where absolutely necessary, the institution avoids the malaise and morale problems that can result from failing to meet a number of its goals. For instance, if the goal were set to double the university's enrollment within ten years but its enrollment only increased by 89 percent, that notable achievement would actually be perceived (both internally by those who work at GCU and externally by its accreditors, donors, and potential students) as a failure. After all, it set a specific goal and didn't achieve it.

Second, the targets established in most strategic plans lack a clear rationale other than a general assumption that bigger is always better or that a school's position in national or international rankings provides genuine insight into its value. It may well be that the investment in infrastructure required to double enrollment would divert resources away from activities that might be more effective at promoting respect, integrity, justice, compassion, and service. It may well be that the higher education landscape ten years from now is so different that a doubling of enrollment, which seems a worthy goal today, actually becomes more of a burden than an asset.

Third, while presidents and governing boards often are motivated by goals tied to increases in size or ranking, other core constituencies—most notably faculty and students—don't find metrics very exciting. As Chip and Dan Heath say in their book *Switch: How to Change Things When Change Is Hard*, "There are some people whose hearts are set aflutter by goals such as 'improving the liquidity ratio by 30 percent over the next 18 months.' They're called accountants" (Heath and Heath, 2010, 82).

Setting specific, quantifiable goals for institutions strikes many professors and students as foreign to what they find most exciting about life and work at a university. And as Adrianna Kezar has noted, "Using concepts foreign to the values of the academy will most likely fail to engage the very people who must bring about the change" (Kezar, 2001, v–vi).

It's no wonder that many faculty members find their eyes glazing over when their presidents regale them with state of the university addresses filled with statistics documenting institutional progress on performance metrics. It would be a very different situation if someone addressed issues they actually cared about, such as respect, integrity, justice, compassion, and service.

That's why GCU's ninth president, Joseph R. Marbach, and the school's board of trustees decided to take a more courageous and visionary approach: instead of setting overly specific goals (that are likely to leave key stakeholders feeling indifferent and uninspired, not be achieved anyway, and prove to be unimportant or even counterproductive even if the school were to be lucky enough to achieve them), they chose a different option.

GCU isn't setting out to be pulled by long-term goals as much as it seeks to be uplifted by its core values. To put it another way, the university isn't going to try to transform itself into yet another research university—much less an R1, that long-outdated Carnegie classification for the highest ranked research university—it's going to be the best version of Georgian Court University that it can be, true to its values and the things it knows it can do well.

YOUR MORAL COMPASS

If entire institutions can have the courage and vision to make that choice, why can't individual academic leaders? In the end, that's where our entire discussion of authentic academic leadership has been taking us. If by now you truly understand who you are as an academic leader and which authentic values define your philosophy of leadership, then why not use those values to set a compass to guide you through the various decisions and difficulties you'll encounter during the months and years ahead?

We're going to use this moral compass as a way of applying our Values-Path-Goal Theory to your growth as an academic leader. To begin with, review the small set of authentic values that you developed in chapter 4. Make sure that you don't have any more than four values on your list. (You can have fewer than four; you just can't have more.)

Of those authentic values, which *one* seems to be the largest contributor to who you are, how you see the world, and how you respond to others? That will be the value that you would never abandon, no matter what the situation and temptation may be. Take that value and go to figure 6.1. Write it down at the top of the compass in the position where on an actual compass you'd find an N or the word *North*. Then take your other authentic values and write those down in the place of the other cardinal points: South, West, and East.

Next, return to the larger list of values you created in chapter 4, the group that we called your core values. Choose the values on this list that you think are most important to you. The goal is that, when your remaining core values are added to your authentic values, you have no more than eight items in total.

Figure 6.1. Your Moral Compass

If you had fewer than four authentic values when you started creating your compass, you can now take the most significant of your core values and complete the cardinal compass points until you're satisfied that, at the four main points of the compass, you've listed the values that are the most important to you as a person.

The remaining four values can then be assigned to the oblique points of the compass where, on an actual compass, the arrows would be pointing southwest, northeast, and so on. When your diagram has all eight values in place, you now have a clear, graphic version of your moral compass.

This visual form of your moral compass is useful in a number of ways. First, when you find yourself in a moral dilemma or quandary, you can pull it out and remind yourself of the direction in which you need to proceed. If, for whatever reason, the value at the top of the compass doesn't provide you with sufficient guidance about what to do, you can consult those other values you wrote down at the cardinal compass points. If even those values don't help you, you still have four more core values that can help you.

Second, even with our best intentions, we all get a bit lost every now and then. We stray from the path of our true selves and do something contrary to our character. Your visual moral compass can point the way out of this undesirable situation. Any direction you choose to go is based on some value that you believe in, that you see as integral to who you are. So, choose the value that best helps you correct the problem, undo the damage, or at least make it less likely that you'll ever make the same mistake again.

Over the years, I've had several different navigation systems in the cars I've owned. In one car, if you happened not to follow the precise directions provided for you by the system, the computerized voice would announce "Recalculating," with what always struck me as something of a sigh of disappointment, before announcing the rerouted path you should take.

The next car did something different. It was the same artificial voice, but, instead of the dire and contemptuous "Recalculating," it announced a chipper "Continue on the current route!" and then proceeded to determine how best to get you to your destination in light of the mistake you made.

A good moral compass should be like the second navigational system. Its purpose isn't to make you feel bad that you make an occasional (or even a frequent) mistake; its purpose is to guide you gently and humanely back toward the destination your better self urged you to pursue.

FROM VALUES TO THE PATH

The third way in which your visual moral compass can be useful is in adopting the Values-Path-Goal Theory that we encountered earlier. Your values, in other words, can become the basis for a system or path that will carry you further in your academic leadership and in your own personal growth.

Let's imagine, for example, that the value you wrote at the top of your moral compass was generosity. Your system or path might be to choose one promising new faculty member each year and devote an hour a week to mentoring that person on how to succeed in the academic world.

You could also resolve to select one charity or cause a month and donate a certain amount of your income to that cause. You could go through your clothing and, every time you buy something new to wear, donate something you don't wear as often to the homeless. (That particular system actually has dual benefits: It helps those in need at the same time that it keeps your closets orderly.)

Whatever system you develop should grow out of one or more values on your moral compass. As you proceed, you'll see how much better this approach is than a simple Path-Goal Approach.

If your goal had been "to be recognized as humanitarian of the year," you might still have gone down the same path of mentoring others, contributing to worthy causes, and donating your clothing. But if you aren't selected for the award that was your goal, you might feel like a failure and end up abandoning your path. With our Values-Path-Goal Approach, you're more likely to stick to your chosen path since it develops naturally from your authentic values.

This Values-Path-Goal concept even works in the case of what others might regard as your flaws or socially unacceptable values. For instance, suppose someone wrote *greed* at the top of his or her moral compass. That person's system might consist of choosing the highest paying job from among all those that are offered, moving on to a better paying position as soon as one comes along, and having a complete stock of excuses ready anytime someone comes along asking for a contribution or a favor that costs money.

That certainly wouldn't be the path or system you'd choose if your key value were generosity, but this system would indeed work for a greedy person and be far better than a goal like "Make at least ten million dollars before the age of thirty." That goal may or may not be reached, but the system would keep working in any case.

Developing a path or system can be a little more challenging if the value at the top of your moral compass is one of the virtues or principles commonly discussed in higher education that appeared in table 2.3. Developing a system based on general virtues like honesty, compassion, and self-control seems pretty straightforward—as does developing a system based on general vices like cowardice, laziness, and selfishness—but what would a system based on academic freedom, collegiality, or faculty-centeredness look like?

In these cases, you have to consider how these academic goals manifest themselves in actual situations. What behaviors distinguish a collegial department chair from a non-collegial department chair or a faculty-centered president from a non-faculty-centered president? Then build your system around those behaviors.

For example, you might say that a dean who is a strong supporter of academic freedom upholds the right of his or her faculty members to teach the material specified in a course syllabus by whatever means his or her professional judgment regards as most appropriate. The dean might also serve as an advocate for the faculty whenever the state legislature or governing board attempts to intrude on matters of academic freedom. And the dean might make a point of including faculty members with dramatically different perspectives on key committees so that people don't lapse into groupthink or assume that they can only reach a conclusion that would please the dean.

Recognizing those behaviors suggests what your system should be as an authentic academic leader. The advantage is that you won't be one of those academic leaders (and unfortunately there are already far too many of them) who gives lip service to ideas like academic freedom and shared governance because they know the faculty likes to hear these terms, but who then acts in ways that are far different from what those values would ordinarily require.

Your path or system will be your means of continuing to improve as an academic leader, advance your career, and develop as the type of person you most want to be. When the pressure of circumstances seems to be encouraging you to make the ends justify the means, your system grounded in your authentic values will provide you with the strategy you need in order to avoid taking a course of action you'll regret later.

THOUGHT EXPERIMENT: PROVOST MONTY BURNS

But should we base a system even on values that others might regard as socially unacceptable?

To explore this idea, let's conduct another thought experiment, this time considering the case of a provost named Monty Burns (who just *happens* to share the name of the despicable power plant owner on the television series *The Simpsons*). In our thought experiment, we'll imagine that Dr. Burns is a generally kind and well-liked administrator who treats everyone—from the chair of the university's governing board to the lowest paid member of the institution's staff—with the utmost respect and understanding.

On several occasions, you've witnessed Dr. Burns respond with genuine pleasure to something as insignificant as a minor report being submitted on time, and you've observed the constructive way he's dealt with deans who have been struggling with challenges in their colleges. He never loses his temper, even when people are obviously at fault for mistakes, and he never makes people feel like failures, even when they're obviously trying to deal with tasks that are far beyond their levels of skill.

As a result, Dr. Burns is the most popular administrator at the university, a three-time recipient of its award for distinguished service, and the recently named Community Humanitarian of the Year.

One semester, you're fortunate enough to accompany the provost to a major national conference. You're looking forward to the opportunities you'll have to observe Dr. Burns's style up close and perhaps to learn a few of his secrets. In fact, over the several days you spend with Dr. Burns at the conference, you feel that he is growing to trust you and to confide in you about his approach to academic leadership.

At dinner one evening, the two of you are alone. You've had a very productive day. The wine that accompanied your meal has made you both a little mellow. And so you feel emboldened to ask the provost openly about his leadership philosophy and administrative goals.

"One of the things I've really admired," you tell Dr. Burns, "is the humanity and kindness you show everyone. For a person of your achievements, you seem to have an amazing level of humility and such a high regard for the people who work at the university. How do you do it? How do you keep from blowing up at someone when that person has made the same mistake five times before? And how do you always remember to show appreciation for even the little things that people do for the university?"

Perhaps the wine has made Dr. Burns even mellower than you assumed or perhaps you really have earned his trust, but the response you receive is both surprisingly candid and completely different from anything you expected.

"I'll let you in on my secret," he begins. "It's a system I developed many years ago, and it's always served me well. You see, I realized that absolutely everyone at the university is a complete and utter idiot. From the president on down, they're completely out of their depth. I'm really the only one who's capable of keeping this university afloat. I have nothing but contempt for each and every student, faculty member, staff member, and donor I meet.

"But do you know what? When I realized that, it was tremendously liberating. I stopped expecting them to be competent and thus stopped becoming frustrated when, yet again, they disappointed me. Now I don't expect anyone to be able to do anything right.

"On those rare occasions when they do accomplish something halfway decent, like meeting the deadline for a report, I'm delighted by the sheer novelty of the situation. Otherwise, I talk to people in gentle tones, like I'd talk to a roomful of ignorant three-year-olds because that's essentially the level at which they perform.

"So, no, I'm never angry or dissatisfied anymore when people do inferior work. That's exactly what I expect of them. How can people let you down when you never thought that they'd get anything right in the first place? That's my system, and it works for me day in and day out."

In this scenario, Dr. Burns shares with you a number of opinions that we might characterize as likely to be socially unpopular. He believes that other people are incompetent, that he alone is responsible for his university's success, and that this situation is unlikely to improve. He even has a system that many would regard as wrong or at least inappropriate.

Perhaps that's the very reason why he shares his system with very few others. But, as he notes, the system does seem to work for him. He says he's used the system for many years, and he's unlikely to have continued to do so if he didn't find it effective.

Even more surprising, the system seems to work for the university: People genuinely like Dr. Burns and appreciate the way he interacts with them. The awards that he received celebrate his service and humanitarian spirit, not because of his values or opinions, but because of the system he uses that directs those values and opinions in a way that helps both the university and him.

We may disagree, even strongly disagree, with Dr. Burns's views, but, at a certain level, that really doesn't matter. If we reflect candidly enough, each of us probably has at least one opinion or perspective on the world that those we work with would reject or perhaps find shocking. As the employee engagement consultant Ron McIntire has noted:

> Acceptance of the fact that we all have some inner darkness, allows us to not be afraid of what others may think of us. It is about knowing that we are not perfect and that we can make mistakes. We learn from our mistakes and ask forgiveness as well as give it. (McIntire, 2016)

If we all shared the same opinion and set of values, the world of higher education would lose its cherished diversity.

But, despite the criticism that conservatives often have of colleges and universities being little more than bastions of liberal groupthink, that simply isn't the case, and we wouldn't want it to be. Higher education depends on students, faculty members, and administrators who bring different worldviews to their shared task of attaining and expanding knowledge.

And although we may be horrified if we knew everything that our colleagues really believe in their heart of hearts, even their most shocking views don't harm and may well benefit the academy when they are part of an overall system of collegial interaction and the pursuit of greater understanding.

"Well, Dr. Burns may have a system," I can imagine a reader saying, "but doesn't his system mean that he's actually not authentic in his academic leadership? I certainly wouldn't give him very high marks for transparency or integrity. And all this talk about systems and paths may be well and good, but it doesn't help me much when my supervisor wants me to set specific goals for the coming year and to develop a strategic plan for my program. I understand the importance of values and the path they suggest, but I can't ignore goals entirely."

No, indeed you can't. Nor should you. The two issues I've imagined our hypothetical reader raising—whether we can truly be authentic when we're not being completely transparent, and how we can reconcile our emphasis on values and systems with the goal-oriented perspective of the modern university—are both important and deserve our thorough consideration. So, let's address them each individually, beginning with the goals component of the Values-Path-Goals Theory that we've been exploring.

FROM THE PATH TO GOALS

To begin with, we need to recognize that the concept of authentic academic leadership doesn't require you to abandon goal-setting entirely; it merely keeps you from putting the cart before the horse.

In most books on management and leadership, even in most books on management and leadership in higher education, we are constantly encouraged to be goal-directed and data-driven. What, these books ask, are you hoping to achieve, and what evidence can you gather to indicate that you're achieving it?

But worthwhile goals should emerge organically from your values and path; they shouldn't be—as so often occurs in traditional Path-Goal Approaches—what *dictate the path*. That's how institutions end up trying to conceal irregularities that resulted in a high graduation rate without students having learned all that much in the process or successful athletic records built on academic or moral malfeasance.

Goals can actually be very useful. They can motivate us, refine our sense of direction, and help us improve our academic programs. But those goals need to be a function of our values and system, not the other way around.

For example, if my value is that taking steps to improve my physical health is important, and if my system is that I only keep wholesome food in my house, then my goal might be to keep my Body Mass Index (BMI) within the healthy range for my height. You might immediately notice something rather counterintuitive about this goal: It lacks most of the characteristics of what are commonly referred to as SMART goals, and it certainly wouldn't pass muster according to the standards we regularly use to evaluate effective course outcomes.

The concept of SMART Goals was first introduced in 1981 by George Doran, Arthur Miller, and James Cunningham as a means of making sure that management objectives were as effective as possible (Doran, Miller, and Cunningham, 1981). The idea is to use the acronym SMART to review your goals so that they're Specific, Measurable, Achievable, Responsible, and Time-Related. Later iterations of the acronym often replaced Achievable with Attainable, Appropriate, Ambitious, and other such words and replaced Responsible with terms like Relevant, Reasonable, and Results-Based. Time-Related is also sometimes rephrased as Timely, Time-Specific, or something similar.

In any case, my goal of maintaining a healthy BMI is certainly not time-specific. When do I intend to reach this objective: next week, next month, or within the next ten years? And although it's somewhat specific, the range of healthy BMIs is fairly broad. The goal isn't the kind of highly precise target that the advocates of SMART Goals often urge us to aim for.

Similarly, this goal falls short of the standards we typically set for outcomes in our academic assessment processes. In my book *The Essential Department Chair*, for instance, I encourage academic leaders to develop learning objectives that set a specific date by when they'll be achieved and include an observable activity that makes attainment of the outcome unmistakable (Buller, 2012, 357).

My health goal doesn't do either of those. It isn't structured as "Within six months, I'll reach a BMI of 22 as calculated by bioelectrical impedance at my doctor's office." That type of outcome is, like SMART Goals, very useful if we want to make some sort of summative judgment. In other words, if you're conducting a program review and you want to know whether you're going to recommend whether a program be maintained on the basis of its quality, having a measurable standard is important.

But as we saw before, goals are (despite every argument made about them during a typical strategic planning process) not very effective as motivators. When my BMI goal is 22, but I only get it down to 24, I feel like a failure and may begin to back away from all the healthy practices that brought my formerly poor BMI down from 41. The very same level of specificity that we find essential in a summative process can be a severe deterrent to progress at other times.

Back in the academic realm, the same principles apply. To return to our earlier example, if a dean's most fundamental value is the support of academic freedom and his or her system is to serve as a faculty advocate and to include a diverse range of perspectives on all faculty committees, then the dean's goals might include such objectives as speaking about the importance of academic freedom to both internal and external stakeholders as often as feasible, reviewing each policy change proposed by the provost through the lens of "Does this proposal reinforce or restrict academic freedom?" and mentoring prospective academic leaders on the importance of academic freedom.

There are no specific timetables associated with these goals, and they may not even be measurable and results-oriented in any traditional sense, but they are far more likely to motivate the dean toward continual personal growth and improvement than goals that merely assess the assessable and quantify the quantifiable. Because they flow seamlessly from the dean's values and chosen path or system, they are goals that the dean is likely to truly care about. As Adams concludes, "goals make sense only if you have a system that moves you in the right direction" (Adams, 2014, 228).

Those goals may not, however, be ones that the *institution* or the dean's supervisors care about. In that case, to meet the requirements of a strategic plan, program review, or evaluation system, the dean may need to restructure his or her personal goals into the format specified by the institution. The goals might have to be assigned a deadline and combined with a specific, observable behavior to satisfy the expectations of the SMART Goals format or a measurable outcomes template.

Any professional work environment is likely to require us to establish objectives that meet certain criteria. But the goals that we publicly express for our program and the goals that we personally establish for our own leadership aren't necessarily identical in any case. We may want our program's graduation rate to improve by 8 percent because that benefits the institution, but we may also want our effectiveness in advocating for academic freedom to improve because that goal flows from our authentic values. Expressing the former goal publicly in no way needs to hinder our pursuit of the latter goal personally.

AUTHENTICITY, TRANSPARENCY, INTEGRITY, AND DISCRETION

I realize that the argument I've just made and the thought experiment of Provost Burns may appear to some like an abandonment of everything we've considered in earlier chapters about being authentic and leading with integrity.

"How is it possible," the objection might go, "for someone to be an authentic academic leader and yet not be transparent about his or her values, opinions, and systems? Shouldn't we assume that integrity is a key component of authenticity? And if an academic leader isn't completely candid about what he or she believes, *particularly* if it is out of concern that some of those opinions might not be socially acceptable or 'politically correct,' how can we possibly regard that person as an authentic academic leader?"

In order to answer these questions and draw together the lessons that I believe to be essential to becoming truly authentic as an academic leader, I believe we need to explore the commonality as well as the differences among four important principles: authenticity, transparency, integrity, and discretion.

The essence of authentic leadership, as I have described it in this book and seen it in action in highly successful academic leaders for the past several decades, is **knowing who you are as a person, particularly with regard to your values, perspectives, personal opinions, and the system you use to apply all of these to your work and life**.

In the words of the former first lady Michelle Obama in her 2015 commencement address at Tuskegee University:

> At the end of the day, by staying true to the me I've always known, I found that this journey has been incredibly freeing. Because no matter what happened, I had the peace of mind of knowing that all of the chatter, the name calling, the doubting—all of it was just noise. . . . It did not define me. It didn't change who I was. And most importantly, it couldn't hold me back. I have learned that as long as I hold fast to my beliefs and values—and follow my own moral compass—then the only expectations I need to live up to are my own. (Obama, 2015)

Her system was to become free from the judgments and condemnations of others by remembering that their misconceptions and animosity didn't define her. That system then generated goals or expectations that she aspired to live up to.

But there's absolutely nothing in this statement about confronting others with those beliefs and values. Authentic leaders thus use their moral compass as a personal guidance system to steer them in the direction they hope to go. They don't misperceive it as a weapon with which they can humiliate others or as a wall that can lead to divisiveness.

Transparency, although a highly desirable complement to authenticity, shouldn't be regarded as identical to it. In terms of values-based leadership, transparency involves accessibility, practical and realistic consistency, and the willingness to share information that affects the lives and work of others.

You might notice my observation that the leader's consistency should be *practical and realistic*. Ralph Waldo Emerson's observation in his essay

Self-Reliance that "A foolish consistency is the hobgoblin of little minds, adored by little statesmen and philosophers and divines" (Emerson, 1857, 50) remains true today. Too much consistency can harden into inflexibility, and wise leaders always know when exceptions to even the strictest of rules are warranted.

Apart from these cases, however, since transparent leaders are guided by a moral compass, they tend to make decisions that are coherent and dependable. You can often predict how they'll respond to different challenges because we've seen their responses before and can recognize a pattern in them. Moreover, transparent leadership can be contrasted to duplicity, the adoption of hidden agendas, and the use of other people as means to a goal instead of as worthwhile ends in themselves.

Transparent academic leaders may well be open and candid about their values and systems when challenged about them, but they don't feel it necessary to share with everyone each thought, opinion, or perspective they have. (I'll have more to say about this point when I discuss discretion in a moment.)

Integrity is a closely related concept. As it was defined in table 2.1, integrity is a commitment to guiding one's behavior with honesty, reliability, and other positive values. Leaders demonstrate integrity when they keep their promises and place the needs of the people they serve ahead of their own. They do the right thing for their organizations, accept responsibility for their actions, and treat people fairly and with respect. They challenge systems and processes that reward irresponsibility, dishonesty, or callous indifference to the rights of others.

But integrity isn't the same thing as authenticity. You can "fake it till you make it" when it comes to integrity, striving for higher ethical standards than you currently possess, but you can't "fake it till you make it" with authenticity. It would be a contradiction in terms. Authenticity requires that you genuinely know your most important values and motivations, and there's no way to simulate that.

You can pretend to be a better person than you are until you eventually truly believe in the values you once claimed to embrace. But if you try to fool yourself into thinking that you're authentic, that very act of self-deception blocks the only pathway you have to genuine authenticity.

Most discussions of authentic leadership assume that, because authentic leaders act with transparency and integrity, they are always completely candid about what they think and how they feel. "What you see is what you get" is a commonly used phrase. (See, for example, Ramsey, 2006, xxii; Crandall, 2007, 169.)

Authentic leaders, the assumption seems to be, "wear their hearts on their sleeves" and are willing to share even their most private reflections with others. In truth, however, this tendency to "let it all hang out" is more characteristic of exhibitionists and narcissists than it is of authentic leaders. A healthy dose of discretion is valuable, not just for authentic academic leaders, but also for all civilized people.

In chapter 5, we explored examples of several socially unpopular opinions that academic leaders may have: atheism, a dislike of pets or children, opposition to the military, and the like. I myself know a few academic leaders (as well as college professors and members of the general population) who share *all* the socially unpopular opinions I just listed.

But it doesn't mean they rub these differences in your face if you happen to disagree with them. They understand that they live in a society where they're in a minority for feeling this way and *unless it's highly relevant to the topic at hand and essential for them to defend a principle they care deeply about*, they're discreet and keep their views to themselves. They understand that, by failing to do so, they wouldn't accomplish anything worthwhile, and they'd just make themselves and others feel bad.

Being authentic is quite a different thing from being a self-confident boor. As Nelson Mandela believed:

> emotions may be authentic, and authenticity is a modern virtue, but one can be authentic without being unnecessarily revealing. . . . [Nevertheless,] [a] noble goal should not be pursued by ignoble means. Practical ones, yes. Venal ones, no. (Stengel, 2010, 99, 234)

The discretion of authentic leaders does not mean, however, that they're not aware of what they believe and why they believe it. Their opinions, even the socially unacceptable ones, might guide their decisions.

For example, when faculty members are advocating for such family-friendly policies as permitting parents to bring their young children to the office or into their classes, they might raise the counterargument that the academic workplace can be an unsafe environment for children or that their presence in the classroom might prove detrimental to effective learning, even though the students might be hesitant to raise this point with those who grade them, write them letters of recommendation, and have their future careers in their hands. These academic leaders might suggest that consideration be given to a childcare center that is at a safe distance from the laboratories and equipment that are critical to the institution's mission and that would not affect pedagogy in the way that children in the classroom might.

In a similar way, they might challenge the notion that military science programs are compatible with the missions of their institution, the belief that every student and faculty member would feel more comfortable and relaxed in a pet-friendly work environment, and that invocations are appropriate in public ceremonies at state institutions.

In these cases, the leaders' convictions, although likely to be highly unpopular, are pertinent to the issues being considered. They're not being shared merely out of a belief that "if I feel it, I have to share it." Authentic academic leaders understand that their views may sometimes cause divisions between themselves and their stakeholders, but they don't pursue divisiveness for its own sake.

All too frequently, a leader's claim just to be speaking his or her mind on the basis that "what you see is what you get" is a thinly veiled excuse not to follow common standards of civilized discourse. It may signal a reluctance to engage seriously with the perspective of others and an unwillingness to change even in the face of compelling evidence that the leader's behavior isn't effective.

"This is who I am: Take it or leave it" is a demand commonly made by those in positions of sufficient power who know that others are going to have to take them as they are, even if doing so is not in the best interest of the group. But, as the executive coach Janet Ioli has observed, "Transparency doesn't translate to authentic communication. . . . Transparency and saying whatever you think doesn't make you empathetic, trustworthy, or able to relate to others" (Ioli, 2015).

Authentic academic leaders recognize the value of their moral compass, but they also recognize that they don't have to be—in fact, should *not* be—100 percent candid with 100 percent of the people they interact with 100 percent of the time. According to Pam Moore, the founder of the social media and digital marketing firm Marketing Nutz, "Authenticity does not require [the] same level of transparency with every relationship" (Moore, n.d.).

The "you" that you share with your significant other is likely to differ from the "you" you share with your coworkers. And that's perfectly fine.

As long as you know who you are, authentic academic leadership doesn't insist that everyone you meet must know your opinion on every possible subject.

All of this brings us back to the hypothetical scenario that began this book. As you'll recall, that case dealt with a department chair who had once had an affair with a student and who is now confronted with a situation where one of his or her faculty members has done the same thing.

The questions we confronted at that time were, "Can the department chair address the current situation without revealing to everyone his or her own past actions? Since that revelation will cause significant harm to the department chair's career and to others whose lives will be affected by this disclosure, is it even right to reveal this long-held secret? In what priority does the department chair respect the demands of morality, effective leadership, honesty, duty, and authenticity in this case?"

Although I provided a partial answer to these questions in chapter 1, it now seems appropriate to revisit the scenario in light of our discussion.

When we first considered the case study, we saw that each action the chair was considering came with a great deal of ethical baggage. After all, the chair had already had the affair and concealed it for many years. Nothing he or she did now could alter that fact.

So, the question then became, "In light of the chair's inability to cancel a past wrongdoing, what is his or her best choice for the future?" As we saw, firing the faculty member would be unacceptable, regardless of whether the chair admitted his or her own misdeeds.

That choice would be hypocritical at best and, if coupled with further deceit that was later exposed, would harm everyone involved in the situation: the chair would probably suffer very severe sanctions; his or her family would be devastated; the faculty member, in addition to having already been terminated, would suffer the indignation of knowing that the person responsible for that decision had been guilty of the very same offense; the faculty, staff, and students of the institution would lose what little respect they may have had for the school's administration; and the institution's own reputation would suffer. Regardless of the system of values that the chair was following, it would be difficult to defend either of these choices.

But it's at this point that we have a real difficulty: Does the chair reveal his or her past affair or not? My answer to this question is unlikely to satisfy those who take a deontological, virtue-based approach to ethical matters, but I believe the only reasonable answer is, "It depends."

What our answer depends on is the chair's authentic values and moral compass. If honesty, candor, transparency, and sincerity are among the chair's highest values—or if the guilt stemming from what he or she had done meant that the chair could no longer tolerate the deception—then the better choice would be to admit what had happened and "face the music."

But if the chair were more utilitarian (the sort of person who was likely to have killed one person to save five lives in the Trolley Problem that we encountered in chapter 4), then discretion might be a better choice than admission of guilt. From a utilitarian or consequentialist perspective, who is better off as a result of the confession? Not the chair who may well lose his or her job. Not the chair's family, which will not only suffer financially from whatever sanctions are imposed on the chair, but will also receive a blow to whatever domestic happiness it currently has. Not the faculty member who had already been granted mercy by the chair. Not the chair's department or institution, which will see a decline in its reputation. Not the student with whom the chair had the illicit relationship, who, if he or she is still alive, would have little reason to have this misconduct from long ago brought to light.

In short, it's very hard to identify any benefit that *anyone* would achieve as a result of this revelation so long after the event. So, unless the chair feels a need to clear his or her conscience, discretion may actually be the better choice.

It's fair to ask whether the approach to ethical leadership that I've just described would have prevented the scandals at the University of North Carolina at Chapel Hill, Pennsylvania State, or any of the other institutions I mentioned in chapter 1. The best answer that I can provide is *probably.*

We have the right to expect academic leaders to adhere to an ethical code; what we don't have the right to do in a diverse and multicultural society is to insist that academic leaders adhere to any *particular* code. To be sure, any responsible academic leader will be guided by an ideal of doing what is best for students, even if that means causing inconvenience or harm to the institution, and to pursue truth wherever it leads us.

And we have the right to ask about these issues when we're interviewing potential academic leaders. (Nevertheless, we might wonder about the effectiveness of such a question. Would someone who didn't care about students or the truth really draw the moral line at lying during an interview?)

It's a reasonable expectation that any academic leader who gives serious consideration to issues of ethics and values will not misappropriate funds for personal gain, condone behavior that harms others, or view the institution's stakeholders largely as a means to an end rather than as ends in and of themselves.

But we can't *guarantee* that these things won't happen. For as long as human institutions exist, there will be those entrusted with those institutions who fail to live up to our expectations for them. Nevertheless, if we want college administrators to be authentic, we must grant them the same right to find inspiration in their own core values that we expect them to grant us in turn.

As I've argued from the very beginning of this book, authentic academic leadership isn't a matter of insisting that administrators are bad people or even just ineffective in their jobs unless they subscribe to some specific code of values. Authentic academic leaders are people who know themselves, understand the values that truly matter to them, and then develop a philosophy of leadership based on those values.

It's pointless to insist that college administrators (or politicians, corporate executives, or anyone else for that matter) be perfect exemplars of moral virtue. Not only is there far too much disagreement about what moral virtue actually is, but human nature is far from flawless.

We lead most effectively when we lead from the entirety of who we are: our faults as well as our merits, our socially unpopular opinions as well as our commonly accepted views, our negative emotions as well as our happiness and warmth, our dark side as well as our bright spots, and our pessimism as well as our optimism.

POSITIVE ACADEMIC LEADERSHIP AND AUTHENTICITY

That conclusion may seem surprising, coming from someone who has written so extensively about positive academic leadership. (See, for example, Buller, 2013.) But as I always tell audiences who come to learn about this topic, positive academic leadership means devoting your energy to the most constructive possible outcome in any situation. It's quite different from endless optimism or the so-called power of positive thinking.

Positive academic leaders can become as frustrated, unhappy, and annoyed as the rest of us. They merely recognize that those feelings can become traps if they yield to them so extensively that they forget how improvement is still possible. They use their frustration, unhappiness, annoyance, and other dark moods as an impetus for making their programs and institutions better. They are, in short, authentic in that they understand who they are and use every aspect of their talents, personalities, and dispositions as tools for their leadership.

While authentic academic leaders may not be positive 100 percent of the time, positive academic leaders are always authentic. Authenticity serves their institutions far more than does strategic planning, outcomes assessment, or any of the other tools or techniques they learn at conferences.

In the end, people don't respond to your technique; they respond to your values. And they want those values to be authentic. Genuine knaves are accepted—they may even be loved—far more than hypocritical saints.

The academic leaders who last aren't necessarily smarter or more virtuous than anyone else. They don't even always have better ideas. But they do stand for something; they recognize the values that form the core of their being, and they put those values into practice. A president, provost, dean, or chair who arrives brandishing a brilliant new vision for the future based on values that he or she doesn't really believe in may appear to succeed for a year or two, or perhaps even three.

But in the end, façades crumble because there's nothing behind them to support them. Once a new leader's honeymoon period is over, it's authenticity and positive academic leadership that will continue to provide momentum. Sheer force of will is no substitute, and top-down management doesn't work at colleges and universities where the real decisions aren't made at the levels that a school's organizational chart might suggest.

I'm probably enough of a postmodernist to remain convinced that principles like honor, integrity, justice, and goodness are social constructs and human creations, not Platonic ideals or standards that owe their existence to anything outside our own consciousness. But even the most confirmed nihilist can recognize the importance that values have in motivating us to "do the right thing" according to whichever definition of *right* we regard as true and in helping academic leaders make the best decisions for the programs entrusted to them.

We can't expect college administrators to believe the same things we believe or act in the same ways we would act if we were in their positions. But we can and should always expect our leaders to lead authentically.

KEY POINTS FROM CHAPTER 6

- Although principle-oriented motivation serves as a corrective to the excessively process- and product-oriented motivation found in higher education, it's possible (not to mention highly desirable) for leaders to pay attention to values, procedures, and goals simultaneously.
- Ultimately, systems are more effective than goals in moving programs and institutions forward. You can pursue a goal but fail to achieve it. As long as you engage in a well-designed and thoroughly considered system, you position yourself for improvement.
- Replacing Robert House's Path-Goal Theory with a Values-Path-Goal Theory makes it less likely that leaders will abandon their core principles in pursuit of an objective.
- Authentic academic leaders often are characterized by their transparency and integrity. But transparency and integrity are not the *same* as authenticity. Authentic academic leaders often understand the importance of discretion and don't feel obliged to share everything they know or feel with every category of stakeholder.
- Authentic academic leaders also practice positive academic leadership, the strategy of seeking the most constructive possible outcome in every situation.

REFERENCES

Adams, S. (2014). *How to fail at almost everything and still win big: Kind of the story of my life*. New York: Portfolio/Penguin.

Adaptive Learning Spaces and Interactive Content Environments (ALICE): North Carolina State University. (n.d.) https://eval.fi.ncsu.edu/adaptive-learning-spaces-and-interactive-content-environments-alice/.

Baumeister, R. F. (1998). Ego depletion: Is the active self a limited resource? *Journal of Personality and Social Psychology. 74*(5), 1252–65.

Buller, J. L. (2012). *The essential department chair: A comprehensive desk reference.* (2nd Ed.). San Francisco: Jossey-Bass.

Buller, J. L. (2013). *Positive academic leadership: How to stop putting out fires and start making a difference.* San Francisco: Jossey-Bass.

Buller, J. L. (2015). *Change leadership in higher education: A practical guide to academic transformation.* San Francisco: Jossey-Bass.

Coffey, T. (January 9, 2012). I am a bitch! *Huffington Post.* http://www.huffingtonpost.com/tabatha-coffey/i-am-a-bitch_b_1194001.html.

Crandall, D. (2007). *Leadership lessons from West Point.* San Francisco: Jossey-Bass.

Doran, G., Miller, A., & Cunningham, C. (November 1981). There's a S.M.A.R.T. way to write management's goals and objectives. *Management Review. 70*(11), 35–36.

Emerson, R. W. (1857). *Essays: First series.* Boston: Phillips, Sampson, and Company.

Heath, C., & Heath, D. (2010). *Switch: How to change things when change is hard.* New York: Broadway Books.

Ioli, J. (August 13, 2015). A lesson from Trump: Is transparency the same as authenticity? http://www.themanagroup.com/a-lesson-from-trump-is-transparency-the-same-as-authenticity/.

Kezar, A. J. (2001). *Understanding and facilitating change in higher education in the 21st century.* Washington, DC: ERIC Clearinghouse on Higher Education.

McIntire, R. (October 30, 2016). Authenticity is not "what you see is what you get." https://www.linkedin.com/pulse/authenticity-what-you-see-get-ron-mcintyre.

Mission and Mercy Core Values: Georgian Court University. (n.d.). http://georgian.edu/mercy-core-values/.

Moore, P. (n.d.). Social brand humanization: Transparency vs authenticity. http://www.pammarketingnut.com/2013/02/social-brand-humanization-transparency-vs-authenticity/.

Obama, M. (2015). Obama's Tuskegee speech too honest for some. http://www.globalblackhistory.com/2015/05/obamas-tuskegee-speech-offends-racists.html.

Peter, L. J., & Hull, R. H. (1969). *The Peter principle.* New York: W. Morrow.

Ramsey, R. D. (2006). *Lead, follow, or get out of the way: How to be a more effective leader in today's schools.* Thousand Oaks, CA: Corwin.

Stengel, R. (2010). *Mandela's way.* New York: Crown.

Trustee Education & Preparation: Valencia College. (2017). http://valenciacollege.edu/trustee-education/valenciasbigideas.cfm.

RESOURCES

Bauman, Z. (1993). *Post-modern ethics.* Oxford, UK: Blackwell.

Bauman, Z. (2006). *Liquid times: Living in an age of uncertainty.* Malden, MA: Polity Press.

Boje, D. M., Gephart, R. P., Jr., & Thatchenkery, T. J. (Eds.). (1996). *Postmodern management and organization theory.* Thousand Oaks, CA: SAGE.

Ferré, F. (2001). *Living and value: Toward a constructive postmodern ethics.* Albany, NY: State University of New York Press.

Haidt, J. (2013). *The righteous mind: Why good people are divided by politics and religion.* New York: Vintage Books.

Klosterman, C. (2016). *But what if we're wrong?: Thinking about the present as if it were the past*. New York: Blue Rider Press.

Schulz, K. (2010). *Being wrong: Adventures in the margin of error*. New York: Harpercollins.

Strom-Gottfried, K. (2016). *Straight talk about professional ethics*. (2nd Ed.). New York: Oxford University Press.

Index

About the Author

Jeffrey L. Buller is the director of leadership and professional development at Florida Atlantic University and has served in administrative positions ranging from department chair to vice president for academic affairs at four very different institutions: Loras College, Georgia Southern University, Mary Baldwin College, and Florida Atlantic University. He is the author of sixteen books on higher education administration, a textbook for first-year college students, and a book of essays on the music dramas of Richard Wagner. Dr. Buller has also written numerous articles on Greek and Latin literature, nineteenth- and twentieth-century opera, and college administration. From 2003 to 2005, he served as the principal English-language lecturer at the International Wagner Festival in Bayreuth, Germany. More recently, he has been active as a consultant to the Ministry of Education in Saudi Arabia, where he is assisting with the creation of a kingdom-wide Academic Leadership Center. Along with Robert E. Cipriano, Dr. Buller is a senior partner in ATLAS: Academic Training, Leadership, & Assessment Services, through which he has presented numerous workshops on college administration, including sessions on authentic academic leadership.

Other Books by Jeffrey L. Buller

The Five Cultures of Academic Development: Crossing Boundaries in Higher Education Fundraising (with Dianne M. Reeves)

Hire the Right Faculty Member Every Time: Best Practices in Recruiting, Selecting, and Onboarding College Professors

Best Practices for Faculty Search Committees: How to Review Applications and Interview Candidates

Going for the Gold: How to Become a World-Class Academic Fundraiser (with Dianne M. Reeves)

World-Class Fundraising Isn't a Solo Sport: The Team Approach to Academic Fundraising (with Dianne M. Reeves)

A Toolkit for College Professors (with Robert E. Cipriano)

A Toolkit for Department Chairs (with Robert E. Cipriano)

Building Leadership Capacity: A Guide to Best Practices (with Walter H. Gmelch)

Change Leadership in Higher Education: A Practical Guide to Academic Transformation

Positive Academic Leadership: How to Stop Putting Out Fires and Start Making a Difference

Best Practices in Faculty Evaluation: A Practical Guide for Academic Leaders

Academic Leadership Day By Day: Small Steps That Lead to Great Success

The Essential Department Chair: A Comprehensive Desk Reference, Second Edition

The Essential Academic Dean: A Comprehensive Desk Reference, Second Edition

The Essential College Professor: A Practical Guide to an Academic Career

More about ATLAS

ATLAS: Academic Training, Leadership, & Assessment Services offers training programs, books, and materials dealing with collegiality and positive academic leadership. Its more than fifty highly interactive programs include the following:

- Introduction to Academic Leadership;
- Team Building for Academic Leaders;
- Time Management for Academic Leaders;
- Stress Management for Academic Leaders;
- Budgeting for Academic Leaders;
- Decision Making for Academic Leaders;
- Problem Solving for Academic Leaders;
- Conflict Management for Academic Leaders;
- Emotional Intelligence for Academic Leaders;
- Effective Communication for Academic Leaders;
- Best Practices in Academic Fundraising;
- Developing Leadership Capacity: How You Can Create a Leadership Development Program at Your Institution;
- We've Got to Stop Meeting Like This: Leading Meetings Effectively;
- Why Academic Leaders Must Lead Differently: Understanding the Organizational Culture of Higher Education;
- Getting Organized: Taking Control of Your Schedule, Workspace, and Habits to Get More Done in Less Time with Lower Stress;
- Collegiality and Teambuilding;
- Change Leadership in Higher Education;
- Promoting Faculty and Staff Engagement;

- Best Practices in Faculty Recruitment and Hiring;
- Best Practices in Faculty Evaluation;
- Best Practices in Coaching and Mentoring;
- Moving Forward: Training and Development for Advisory Boards;
- Training the Trainers: How to Give Presentations and Provide Training the ATLAS Way;
- Managing Up for Academic Leaders: How to Flourish When Dealing with Your Boss and Your Boss's Boss;
- Creating a Culture of Student Success;
- Positive Academic Leadership: How to Stop Putting Out Fires and Start Making a Difference;
- Authentic Academic Leadership: A Values-Based Approach to Academic Leadership;
- Mindful Academic Leadership: A Mindfulness-Based Approach to Academic Leadership;
- Fostering a College University: An In-Depth Exploration of Collegiality in Higher Education;
- Managing Conflict: An In-Depth Exploration of Conflict Management in Higher Education;
- A Toolkit for College Professors;
- A Toolkit for Department Chairs;
- Exploring Academic Leadership: Is College/University Administration Right for Me?

ATLAS offers programs in half-day, full-day, and multiday formats. ATLAS also offers reduced prices on leadership books and sells materials that can be used to assess your institution or program:

- the Collegiality Assessment Matrix (CAM), which allows academic programs to evaluate the collegiality and civility of their faculty members in a consistent, objective, and reliable manner;
- the Self-Assessment Matrix (S-AM), which is a self-evaluation version of the CAM;
- The ATLAS Campus Climate and Morale Survey;
- The ATLAS Faculty and Staff Engagement Survey.

These assessment instruments are available in both electronic and paper formats. In addition, the free ATLAS E-Newsletter addresses a variety of issues related to academic leadership and is sent free to subscribers.

For more information, contact:
ATLAS: Academic Training, Leadership, & Assessment Services
4521 PGA Boulevard, PMB 186
Palm Beach Gardens, FL 33418
800-355-6742; www.atlasleadership.com
E-mail: questions@atlasleadership.com

89298744R00123

Made in the USA
Middletown, DE
15 September 2018